Marijuana 101

Professor Lee's Introduction to

Growing Grade A Bud

Green Candy Press

Marijuana 101: Professor Lee's Introduction to Growing Grade A Bud by Professor Lee.
Published by Green Candy Press
www.greencandypress.com

ISBN 978-1-937866-88-4
eBook ISBN 978-1-937866-89-1

Photography: Cover photo: Kyle's Special Blend © by Andre Grossman. Back cover photographs are copyright © Andre Grossman, Sweet Seeds, and Green Born Identity. Interior photographs are copyright © by 420Clones.com, All Good Medibles, Alpine Seeds, Andre Grossman, Autofem Seeds, BC Bud Depot, BC Northern Lights, Ch9 Female Seeds, David Strange, Delicious Seeds, Delta 9 Labs, Dinafem Seeds, Dr. Greenthumb Seeds, Dutch Passion, Ed Borg, Eva Female Seeds, Giorgio Alvarezzo, Green Born Identity, Green Devil Genetics, Green House Seed Co., Growl LED systems, HID Hut, Humboldt Nutrients, KC Brains, LF Imaging, Low Life Seeds, MG Imaging, Ministry of Cannabis, mmJars.com, Mr. Nice Seeds, No Mercy Supply, OGA Seeds, OriginalSeeds.org, Paradise Seeds, Peak Seeds, Pepper Design, Sagarmatha Seeds, Samsara Seeds, Sativa Steph, Sensi Seeds, Serious Seeds, SinsemillaWorks!, Stoney Girl Gardens, Subcool, Sweet Seeds, Team Green Avengers, The Pot Father, Trichome Technologies, Vulkania Seeds, Weado, weed.co.za, and World of Seeds.

Printed in China by 1010 Printing.
Massively distributed by P.G.W.

Foreword

This book was written for those who know nothing at all about growing. Whether you're a consumer simply interested in knowing how marijuana is grown, or a potential grower looking to begin a simple, small operation that yields a great one-time crop or even a personal sea of perpetual buds, you've picked the right tutor. I ran garden after garden for over ten years, keeping myself stoned to high heaven, and most importantly, I got away with it. Now that enough years have passed, I feel safe in sharing my knowledge with you, using my personal notes and insights to help you get your grow off the ground.

First, however, I'm going to have to set some rules before you go off half-cocked and paint yourself into a corner. Try to forget everything some supposed expert slurred to you during a hazy conversation. While it is possible that they knew what they were talking about, it's just as possible that they were full of crap. Regardless of their intent, it's a fact of growing that what may have worked for them might not be the best thing for you. My goal in this book is to help you avoid all the basic beginner mistakes and unnecessary expense, and to figure out the best set-up for you to make it work the first time.

Please don't start any garden without first reading your way through this book; it's not that big and won't take too long. Spend some time concentrating on the parts that show garden examples and types of growing systems. Think about where you could grow and what types of problems you may encounter in terms of light, noise, air ventilation, smell, and security.

You may have already tried a blind hand at cultivating and been confused at why you haven't met with the results you anticipated; that's fine, I'm not mad at you. Hell, that's how I got started. My first plants suffered horrible fates and I get a little weepy thinking about all the bud that wasn't. However, I've learned from both my positive and negative experiences, and have put every piece of useful advice I can think of into this book, trimming out as much technical jibber jabber as possible. They don't hand

out professorships lightly, so trust me, follow my suggestions, and we'll turn your initial shortcoming into bowls and spiffs a-plenty.

Yours truly,
Professor Lee

About the Author

Professor Lee has spent years perfecting his growing skills and has earned himself considerable esteem in the academic world as well as two green thumbs along the way. Starting out like most novice growers, totally ignorant of what marijuana plants needed to thrive, his first active attempt was made in a toy chest with a two-foot fluorescent light screwed to the inside lid, no ventilation, and a two-inch deep pot filled with yard dirt. The poor plants had no chance whatsoever, and managed to grow just a few scrawny inches before giving up on life completely. Instead of turning his back on growing, he threw himself into research, and after a twenty dollar investment in potting soil, a bucket, and some aluminum foil, he managed to grow a scraggly six-foot tree covered with small sweet buds in his bedroom window. Puffing away on the first of many homegrown joints, he made the decision that started a decade-long obsession: it was time for him to make a serious attempt at growing some real weed!

The quest began small and simply, with some cheap four-foot fluorescent lamps and soil-filled containers, which resulted in his first sea of green: a true thing of beauty. Inevitably, he made a few mistakes, but harvested close to an ounce of primo homegrown bud and a pile of cheap B-grade leaf smoke. After several successful crops growing mostly sativa plants, Prof. Lee (or plain old Mr. Lee, as he was known then) acquired his first indica plant, which radically changed his approach to growing and led to his education in cloning and rotation crops.

Just one year later, he had a continuous system that kept him in perpetual smoke, but he continued to tweak the system and add new genetic material, making mistakes and gaining great insight. He made pilgrimages to meet those who really knew the craft—talking, smoking and learning from them. Between standing in immense gardens that earned a million dollars a year, and watching novice growers smoke their first crop that cost next to nothing to grow and brought nothing more than a good time and a case of the munchies, he began to

About the Author

appreciate the true love of marijuana cultivation in all its forms. He tried all the most popular systems, from sunlight in windows and grow lights in closets to hydroponics systems with diluted nutrient feeds and "hippy" organic soil-based systems. He spent years fighting insects, fungus, heat, and nutrient problems galore, until he perfected what he believed to be the best method: a rotation system of clones that involved little maintenance and only two days a month doing something that resembled real work. After years of intensive work, he finally found himself in a position to sit in his garden smoking bowl after bowl of homegrown and watching the green grass grow.

Unfortunately, all great things must come to an end. Having earned the title of Professor, Mr. Lee retired, got married, and chipped away at this book. He cites no regrets, having never been caught, but more importantly he came away from his growing career believing that anyone can grow marijuana, and that one day we all should be legally allowed to do so. After what can only be described as a long, strange trip, all that remains is for him to spark up a fat one and impart his wisdom to you, his new student.

Dedication

Everyone needs help from time to time and authors are no exception. My greatest thanks go to the Dallas Crew, consisting of my good friends and ex-roommates who tolerated my gardens as well as everything else that I put them through. They often edited my drafts, helped with photo shoots, and smoked many quality control samples with me. In no particular order they are AD, BG, TS, DS, RR, SG, MF, JD, Big D, and last but certainly not least BF.

I also want to give a very special thanks to all the fine folks up in British Colombia, Canada who let me into their wonderful gardens and places of business, even though I was a "stupid American"! Finally, many thanks to all those other anonymous growers who didn't want to have any mention of themselves in this book, but did let me into their secret gardens to photograph their beautiful plants.

Professor Lee

Contents

Lesson 1

The Technical Stuff

Potology 101

Listen up, class: this book is written for the beginner grower, so consider this the start of your education. Before we dive in, though, I have to emphasize that despite the fact that there are more people growing marijuana in the United States than ever before, it is still illegal. The decision to grow or not to grow is yours alone to make, but my best suggestion is this: if you do decide to grow, keep it small and keep it secret. Are you staying? OK, then let's start from the beginning.

Marijuana: An Overview

What exactly is pot? What have I been smoking all these years?

Pot, also known as weed, chronic and cannabis, is nothing more than the dried flowers and leaves of the marijuana plant.

Why does it get me high?

The "high" that you feel from smoking marijuana happens thanks to **cannabinoids**, which are produced by the plants and contain tetrahydrocannabinol (THC). THC is a naturally occurring psychoactive substance that can be found in the tiny white **trichomes** covering marijuana buds, and is responsible for the fuzzy head feelings and fits of giggling that we all know and love.

What exactly do the buds consist of?

Buds are dense collections of the small female flowers of the marijuana plant. There may be hundreds or thousands of individual flowers in a good size bud. Larger top-growing collections of buds are called colas.

What are those little red hairs?

The hairs are called pistils and they are part of the female flower. At the base of each set of pistils is a little oval pod where the seed grows if the plant is pollinated.

CH_3

OH

H_3C

H_3C O C_3H_{11}

Tetrahydrocannabinol

THC is the main psychoactive chemical that gets one high.

After harvest, THC can be degraded by heat, light, and exposure to air. There are a few other active ingredients in marijuana that may or may not affect people. The most common is tetrahydrocannabivarin THCV, a form of THC. This provides an instant power high, yet only lasts about 30 minutes. Cannabinol CBN, cannabichromene CBC, and cannabidiol CBD are also found in weed, though they have little, if any, effect. When THC degrades it converts into these lower quality CBs.

What is hemp?

Hemp is the industrial name for marijuana; it is what they make textiles, paper, oils, plastics, shoes, and other stuff from. Generally hemp has very little, if any, of the psychoactive chemicals that get one high. You could smoke a whole field of the stuff and only get a mild headache.

What is cannabis?

Cannabis is the technical name for pot. There are three species of cannabis: sativa, indica, and ruderalis. The first two are the most popular for growing, and ruderalis has largely fallen out of favor because of its low levels of THC. Indica and sativa buds produce different highs when smoked, and have very different properties in terms of growing: sativa plants grow fairly tall, while indica plants are smaller and bushier.

There are numerous strains, or breeds, of cannabis, with new ones being developed all the time. Some strains, such as the pungent Skunk, are crossbreeds of indica and sativa plants, while others are pure breeds of one or the other.

Does medical marijuana really work?

Having researched the subject extensively, my professional opinion is that yes, it does. However, the small minority faking illnesses to get a little weed are causing medical marijuana to lose its respectability. There are many great online resources covering this topic; it's best to research and make up your own mind.

Should marijuana be legal?

Given that it is known to cause less physical damage to users than legal drugs like alcohol and tobacco, and that its status as a controlled substance forces users to interact with drug dealers who might encourage them to try other drugs, I believe that yes, marijuana should be legalized.

Most of the arguments against the legalization of pot are actually arguments against the use of pot, which will carry on regardless of the law. Also, legalizing and taxing marijuana in the same manner as tobacco would funnel a lot of money back into the struggling US economy, and make us all a lot more comfortable (in more ways than one!).

The Life Cycle of Marijuana Plants

Like most seeds, marijuana seeds sprout and begin to establish themselves in spring, with the arrival of warmer and wetter conditions. The first leaves to emerge are embryonic; complete, single-bladed leaves with smooth edges. The next set are also

Seedlings will quickly begin to crowd each other. Be prepared to transplant them to larger containers.

Plant Structure

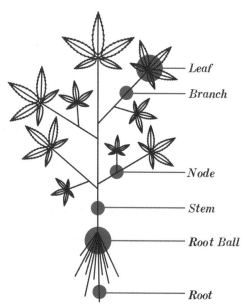

Leaf

Branch

Node

Stem

Root Ball

Root

single-bladed, but have serrated edges. With each new set of leaves, the number of blades increases two at a time: 3, 5, 7, and so on. The maximum number of blades the leaves will produce depends on the plant's genetics, environment, and diet.

During spring and early summer the plants grow the fastest. This phase is known as the vegetative growth stage, and at this point the plants are trying to grow as big and strong as they can. The stronger they are, the more flowers and seeds they can make.

Starting in mid to late summer or early fall, the plants undergo the physiological changes that prepare them for flowering. This is called pre-flowering; it's similar to puberty in humans. During pre-flowering, the plants' overall growth slows down and the internodes begin to form in a zigzag pattern. This way, the developing buds create a larger surface area, which increases the female's chance of catching some stray pollen on the wind.

The actual flowering cycle begins when the first true flowers bloom. Flowering lasts between six and 12 weeks, depending on the strain. Marijuana is **dioecious**, meaning that normally a plant will be entirely male or female, although **hermaphroditic** mutations do occur. Females are the desired plants when growing for smoking, because they produce the largest collections of smokable buds, while the males, in comparison, produce few. Unfertilized female plants, known as sinsemilla, produce the most weight, but growing them requires a degree of patience, as they can take much longer to finish.

Reproduction occurs when male pollen impregnates female flowers and seeds are produced. The plants drop the seeds, the parents die, and all hope for future generations lie with the seeds through the winter. To create sinsemilla plants, which yield more buds and more THC, pot growers avoid letting pollination occur.

Considerations

Before you plant your first seed or spend your first dollar, it is a good idea to sit down and think through your decision. Here are a few points to consider.

1. Is growing right for you?

Do you really want to be considered one of the "bad guys"? In 2007, between 800,000 and 900,000 people in the United States were arrested for marijuana-related charges. Despite the current administration's more positive stance on medical marijuana being an enormous step towards a sane national drug policy, we must remember that the war is not yet won, and that policy shifts have a tendency

Lesson 1.1: *Potology 101*

From Seed to Smoke

Seeds from Ch9 Female Seeds.

Sprouts.

OGA Seeds young seedling.

Young plant.

Plant.

Young flowers.

Ready for harvest.

Dried bud.

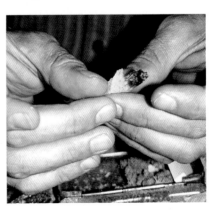
Final product.

Don't Get Ahead of Yourself

My first successful crop was grown in a brightly lit upstairs window. Total expenses were twenty dollars for some potting soil, fertilizer, aluminum foil, and twine. I recycled an old sand pail for the container and used a foil curtain strung up with the twine to reflect extra light. Even after I upgraded to a simple hydroponics system and a few fluorescents, the investment cost was nominal.

Trichomes and pistils are bountiful on these plants from Alpine Seeds.

to come and go. In a perfect world we would all be free to grow and enjoy magical forests of lush buds without the fear of incarceration, but sadly when deciding whether to grow or not we still need to wrestle with the obvious risk versus reward factors. Growing marijuana is a dangerous business, and carries risks no matter how much discretion you use.

2. What do you hope to achieve?

This book is geared towards the self-sufficient user that wants to dabble in a crop or two, or set themselves up with a small garden that will supply them with a steady reliable supply. I strongly advise against trying to grow a thousand pounds your first time. Not only does it increase your chances of being caught, but also it is truly unrealistic. Most amateurs don't have what it takes to pull off a major grow operation, and most veterans know better than to run the risk. Remember that gardens don't have to be massive undertakings with mounds of expensive equipment. I suggest that you start off simple and gain experience before investing too much.

3. Do you really have what it takes to grow?

To be successful in growing, more than anything else, you need to be a particular type of person: an operator. This is a person who does what they have to do every single time. In the world of a pot grower one slip up can potentially result in arrest or rip off, so if you aren't confident in your abilities, don't grow.

4. Do you have the time and inclination to look after marijuana plants?

Growers have a duty to be responsible caregivers to their plants. Much like children, they are totally dependant on you for survival. You should be ready to follow a strict schedule and take a daily interest in their well being, as plants need care and attention to produce the best results. It is up to you alone to meet their needs. If you do so, your plants will do the rest.

The basic needs of marijuana plants are similar to your own: light, water, nutrients, and air. Much like you, though, plants find that a few optional extras can make their lives a little more comfortable. Just as you need a roof over your head to ward off the elements, your plants need a proper home to keep them safe from predators. Just as you thrive though exercise, your plants will become stronger and more productive if they have some good air circulation to strengthen their stems. Just as hygiene is essential for your health, your plants need to be cleaned regularly to avoid dust collecting on their leaves and clogging the pores that absorb air.

Chapter Summary

Growing marijuana is a risky business, and highly illegal. Do you really have what it takes to be a "bad guy" in the eyes of the law, and keep it secret from your friends and family?

The three species of cannabis are sativa, indica and ruderalis. Research which species or crossbreed will suit you and your grow space best.

Cannabis plants move through these stages: sprouting, vegetative growth, pre-flowering, flowering, reproduction and harvest.

THC is the main psychoactive ingredient that gets you high.

Terms to Learn
- Sinsemilla
- Sativa
- Indica
- Ruderalis
- THC

Security

Once you've made the decision to grow, the most important thing to think about is security. There are many factors such as light, smell, gossip, and garbage that can make one a victim of thieves, or worse, cops. Here are some security factors to consider.

Location

It is essential to find is a secure area in which to grow your garden; someplace that allows you to control who has access. Very few people are lucky enough to own land which is totally secure, so indoor grow spaces are always preferable in terms of security. Thankfully, horticulture has moved through countless stages of development since man first began to farm, and the advancements in artificial light in the last few decades have finally allowed marijuana cultivation to move indoors.

Previously, you had to grow your crop when the sun permitted, and if you smoked your stash before next year's harvest you were out of luck. Nowadays, with a modest investment in money and space, an indoor grower can produce a perpetual harvest for as long as they wish, and feel a little safer while they do so.

For marijuana growers, the first real breakthrough came with the successful application of more powerful **HID** (High Intensity Discharge) lamps. The subsequent introduction of indica strains that could make the most of indoor lighting added to the productivity of closet gardens. Up until this point, growers often met with mediocre results using sun-loving sativa breeds and row after row of weak fluorescent tubes.

I would recommend an indoor set-up for any new grower, and basements or upstairs bedroom closets are great choices. Sometimes a grower has no choice but to grow in a relatively vulnerable place like a living room window. These higher-risk areas are best for small gardens of one or two plants that can be easily moved into a hiding place when necessary.

Larger gardens usually give themselves away with noise or smell, so it's a great idea to employ a good ventilation system, ion generators, and/or air fresheners to deal with the smell. When visitors come over turn off anything that creates noise or

BC Northern Lights

The security of your grow is very important. If you feel that you can't build a sufficiently clandestine grow room, think about investing in a pre-made system. The Producer from BC Northern Lights is an extremely secure hydro system offering odor control via a cocoa carbon filter, and Lumatek Digital Ballasts that keep power consumption lower than most household appliances.

Warning!

Never dispose of marijuana leaves and plant parts with your regular garbage. If the cops find your electric bill and old bank statements mixed in with growing garbage, then you've got problems. By keeping your garden trash separate from your regular trash and disposing of things properly, you might just save yourself from being robbed or doing some jail time.

light, and lock the door to the garden. Plants begin to smell as soon as they sprout, and marijuana can have a very noticeable odor. In a week you will notice the smell drifting around the room; in a month the house could draw cops like a ripe corpse draws flies. The chapter on atmosphere gives details about dealing with this and related problems.

Traffic

This refers to your coming and goings. Dragging bag after bag of soil and manure into your place in full view of the neighbors or a landlord is a dead give away, and the box from the hardware store with the picture of the HID lamp doesn't help either. Think ahead, and put an empty cardboard box in your car's trunk to load at the store. I would never advise anyone to transport large quantities of fresh homegrown, live plants, or any amount of marijuana in conjunction with grow supplies.

For smoking purposes you should only ever carry enough to meet your immediate needs. Never carry paraphernalia like pipes, extra papers, or anything with residue on it. I can and have very quickly disposed of a dry, shitty-tasting joint while being pulled over.

Trash

When growing marijuana, you have to seriously think about your garbage.

After unsmokable leaves have been used to make something edible, such as hash butter, you still have to deal with a wad of soggy green leaf matter and everything else from the harvest that you are not going to consume. Left over leaf matter and stems should be buried in a compost pile or put down the garbage disposal, as flushing leaves down a toilet might find you in jail holding a plumber's bill and burning them in a fireplace can alert the entire neighborhood to your little hobby. If you cannot find a way to destroy materials like root masses and mediums then the best way to dispose of them is to place them in a couple of layers of plastic grocery bags and then inside a paper sack or cardboard box. The plastic bags will reduce the chance of smell or leaks while the paper bag will hide the contents from prying eyes. Dispose of these packages discreetly, and use gloves to avoid leaving fingerprints.

Yourself

The biggest security leak in your life as a grower can actually be yourself. It's

This healthy harvest was created using a BC Northern Lights grow station which helps growers maximize their yields.

Keep your smoking paraphernalia as secret as your grow room. The less people see, the better!

Tip!

Even if you only have access to pure sativa strains like Mexican, you can still grow some respectable buds under a mid- to high-range HID lamp.

natural to feel guilty about not hooking your friends up, but having people ask, "Is it ready yet?" will get on your nerves very quickly, especially if the question is coming from an ever-growing circle of "friends" and acquaintances. Keeping everyone in the dark gives you the option of safely growing again, or maintaining a perpetual harvest for years; the less people know, the better. Ideally, only one person should know about your grow and that's you. If the wrong person finds out about your garden, you may find yourself being ratted out or robbed. My

Lesson 1.2: *Security*

Strains like this Nepalese Dragon from Ministry of Cannabis are quite pungent and you need a good air filtration system to hide the smell.

humble opinion is this: if their name isn't on the property lease, then they don't need to know.

An oversight on your part is much more likely to give you away than a narc. A ray of stray light at three o'clock in the morning or a curious smell can alert everyone to your efforts and be as conspicuous as a neon sign saying "POT GROWING HERE." Always be aware of this.

Chapter Summary

Consider these factors when starting your grow:

Location: find a secure indoor grow space that you can control access to.

Traffic: ensure that your frequent comings and going won't arouse unwanted suspicion.

Trash: always separate grow garbage from regular garbage and dispose of it properly.

Yourself: keeping your grow operation secret isn't easy, but it is essential to keep your stash secure and yourself out of jail. Tell no one.

Terms to Learn

- HIDs
- Organic
- Non-organic

Nutrients

Ensuring that your marijuana plants are getting the correct nutrients is essential to your growing success. If your soil isn't providing the plants with sufficient amounts of the three most important nutrients, then it may be necessary to help them out with a fertilizer.

Nutrient content is listed on fertilizer containers; look for a label marked "N-P-K." This stands for nitrogen (N), phosphorus (P), and potassium (K), which are the most common elements used by most plants. Nurseries and grow stores carry NPK testing kits and battery-powered probes to accurately measure the levels of each substance in soil or water. These range in price, but usually fall between ten and twenty dollars.

How do I know if my plants have nutrient deficiencies?

There's old saying that goes something like this: "If it ain't broke, don't fix it." Strange as it might sound, this is a great guideline for marijuana cultivation. If your plants are growing quickly with lush green leaves then all is fine. Purple tinting of leaves and stems may confuse you if they appear on your apparently healthy plant, but some strains may naturally develop these traits, so if the rest of the plant is healthy, don't worry. Likewise, don't freak out at the first yellow leaf you find. Plants often shed older leaves that have served their purpose. The only time you should become nervous is when the plants are runted, turn pale yellow, or develop **chlorosis** or **necrosis**. If this happens, it's time to step in.

To better understand nutrient deficiencies you should become familiar with two basic symptoms. The first is chlorosis: a spotty yellowing or whitening of leaves. You should always be on the lookout for this, as it's often the first hint of a problem. If you act accordingly, chlorosis can be reversed in a few weeks. If ignored, it will spread over the entire leaf. The second symptom is necrosis: dead tissue. There is no way to cure this once it happens. Necrosis may follow or accompany chlorosis.

NPK levels, however, are not your only concern when it comes to nutrients.

Chlorosis occurring between the veins of the leaf.

Necrosis on the outside edges of the leaf.

Tip!

Never buy a fertilizer or product that contains any form of herbicide. This is otherwise known as weed killer, and it really will kill your weed.

All plants, including marijuana, use other chemical nutrients as well as the ones discussed above; these are called the secondary elements and microelements. Most fertilizers list these, as well as the source that they came from. As long as they are listed you should never have a problem.

The Major or Macronutrients

Nitrogen (N)

Plant Use: Nitrogen is one of the most important nutrients. It helps make chlorophyll, which the plants need to make their food. Nitrogen is needed most during the vegetative part of the plant's life cycle.

Lesson 1.3: *Nutrients*

Nitrogen deficiencies are the most common problem in marijuana cultivation, simply because marijuana is so dependent on it. Most growers will have to fertilize several times during the plant's life to meet its needs.

Deficiency Symptoms: Signs of deficiency include smaller leaves, slowed growth, a red or purple tinge on the stems and petioles, and yellowing of the leaves. This will most commonly start with the lowest fan leaves and then move up towards the actively-growing shoots, which will be similarly affected.

Phosphorus (P)

Plant Use: This element is associated with root and floral development. Most growers change the nutrient levels prior to the plant's flowering cycle.

Deficiency Symptoms: Vegetative growth may develop a dark dull green or blue green color. The stems, petioles and undersides of leaves can have a red or purplish tinge, and the leaf margins on lower leaves develop a downward curl. These leaves should fall off easily.

Potassium (K)

Plant Use: This is used by plants for everything from enzymes to breathing. Lack of potassium is very rarely a problem, except in acidic soils or low-light gardens.

Deficiency Symptoms: Starting at the bottom of the plant the undersides of leaves develop necrosis between the veins, along with rusty or gray tips and blade margins. Leaves may also be dull green or blue-green.

The Secondary Nutrients

Calcium (Ca)

Plant Use: Calcium is essential as it helps the plants absorb nutrients and develop roots. Deficiency is rarely a problem, however, since it's a component of most common fertilizers.

Deficiency Symptoms: Plants not receiving enough calcium may become dark green and have very slow growth. Severely deficient plants have twisted or discolored shoot tips and bud sights, which are usually yellow or purple.

Sulfur (S)

Plant Use: Plants use sulfur to help create various proteins, enzymes, and other cellular components.

Deficiency Symptoms: A lack of sulfur results in the yellowing of the newest shoots

Good collection of nutrients and fertilizers.

Macronutrient, Secondary Nutrient, and Micronutrient Deficiencies

Nitrogen deficiency.

Phosphorus deficiency.

Potassium deficiency.

Magnesium deficiency.

Sulfur deficiency.

Copper deficiency.

Zinc deficiency.

Manganese deficiency.

Iron deficiency.

and leaves at the top of the plant. Eventually the whole plant may turn pale or limish in color.

Magnesium (Mg)

Plant Use: This is used in the production of chlorophyll, so is necessary for the plant to make food, and is also an ingredient for many enzymes. Magnesium is the only secondary nutrient that may cause you any problems.

Deficiency Symptoms: When the plant doesn't have enough Mg, its leaves turn yellow, followed by the shoots. A drop or two of liquid detergent should treat any Mg problems you may have.

The Micronutrients

If these are listed on the fertilizer container you should never have a problem.

Boron (B)

Plant Use: Boron is required for good root development, and slows the absorption of oxygen in leaf tissue.

Deficiency Symptoms: Too little boron causes a reduction in the development of flowers.

Copper (Cu)

Plant Use: Copper aids in enzyme activity and in metabolism of carbohydrates.

Deficiency Symptoms: When a copper deficiency is present, the top leaves wilt and the plant's overall color fades.

Iron (Fe)

Plant Use: This is found in respiratory enzymes, and aids in the process of photosynthesis. It is essential for the formation of chlorophyll.

Deficiency Symptoms: Starting with the bottom leaves, white chlorosis will appear between the veins, often becoming necrotic. Leaves may become completely white with brown margins and tips.

Manganese (Mn)

Plant Use: Manganese aids enzyme activity, and also helps photosynthesis occur.

Deficiency Symptoms: Starting with the top leaves chlorosis and necrosis develops. Stems may yellow and turn woody.

Tip!

When sprouting, use nutrient-clear pH-balanced water. I would often add a capful of some sprouting formula to a gallon of water, to give my plants a little push.

Organic fertilizers and nutrients are available in a wide range of commercial products.

Zinc (Zn)

Plant Use: Zinc is present in many enzymes within a plant, and also helps preserve chorophyll.

Deficiency Symptoms: Too little zinc leads to chlorosis or necrotic spots, and eventual shedding of the affected leaves. White chlorosis will appear between the veins of the bottom leaves first.

Organic Fertilizers

The benefits of organic growing are the subject of much discussion. While it is widely agreed that organic systems present unique challenges and make it more difficult to grow a substantial crop, the health and environmental benefits often lead people to go down this route. Some people also claim that organic buds taste better than non-organic ones. In addition, soil-based growing is a lot more forgiving than, for example, a hydroponics system, as soil can handle overfeeding or excess nutrients better, and so can be useful for a first-time grower.

For those who don't want to use chemical fertilizers, the following natural organic fertilizer sources are readily available at most nurseries.

Manure

The most common types of manure are cow and chicken. Cow manure is available in bulk amounts for reasonable costs, while a five-pound bag of chicken manure costs about forty dollars and has an average NPK ratio of 4-2-2. Don't use too much manure, or the soil will remain soggy and the pH level will be affected. Be sure to cover the top of the medium with an inch or two of plain soil to prevent fungus and insects from discovering the manure.

Fish Emulsion

Emulsion, or as it is better known, fish shit, has a nice low NPK level; commercial brands usually run 5-1-1 or 5-2-2. The best way to apply emulsion to your grow is to dissolve a teaspoon in a gallon of water and feed this concoction to the plants every two or three weeks. Do not use in a hydroponics system, as it will build up on the container walls and stink.

Bat Guano

Guano is bat droppings, and it is mined all over the world as a valuable fertilizer. The pH and nutrient levels of guano depend on the health and diet of the bats it

Lesson 1.3: *Nutrients*

came from. Most guano is a little higher in phosphorus than nitrogen, making it a wonderful fertilizer for the flowering stage.

Seaweed or Kelp

Processed seaweed or kelp fertilizers usually come in liquid forms that are added to the water at feeding time. The NPK levels are very low, so overdosing on seaweed is unlikely.

pH

pH stands for "presence of hydrogen," and it is basically a measurement of acidity or alkalinity. Many different things can affect the pH of your garden, so it is best to test the pH levels often and adjust the soil accordingly.

The complete pH range runs from 0 to 14, with 0 being the most acidic and 14 the most alkaline. Marijuana can only absorb nutrients in a pH range of about 5.5 to 7.5, which is fairly narrow. Either extreme is undesirable. For hydroponically grown plants, I suggest a level of about 6.2, but for soil-based gardens a higher level of around 6.8 is preferred. pH adjusters come in two forms: acid and alkaline. These adjusters raise or lower the pH level to the preferred point. Nutrients, some container types, and even some mediums can affect pH levels so an amount of fine-tuning is almost always necessary. For instance, if a plant growing in a perfectly balanced medium is being watered with heavily alkaline water, then over time the medium's pH would be raised.

A pH tester gauges the acidity or alkalinity of the water. These testers come in a variety of types and can be picked up at grocery stores, nurseries, and pool stores. Head shops that cater to marijuana growers often over price these products, but it can be helpful to go to one, see what brands they carry then shop around for the same thing elsewhere.

The easiest pH adjusters to use are the pre-dissolved liquid kinds that can be added to water. Use caution when handling these types as they can easily burn you; rubber gloves and strong ventilation are fundamental safeguards. Solid adjusters like lime dust or wood ash can be added to soil-based systems.

Learning how to mix chemicals and nutrients takes practice, so take your time and follow the directions on the packaging. After you have worked out the correct ratios for your situation, then the entire process becomes fast and easy. Using a mixing container can speed it up even more.

If you can't locate store-bought pH adjusters, alternatives can sometimes

Older leaves can naturally turn yellow.

Purple coloration can be natural.

Untreated chlorosis spreads quickly.

Fix!

If you accidentally add too much fertilizer, then the only way to save the plants is to remove a few inches of medium off the top and replace it with new medium, and then slowly run several gallons of lukewarm pH-balanced, nutrient-free water through the containers to flush out the excess nutrients. If successful, the plant will return to healthy growth. Don't fertilize them again!

be found around the house. Water that is too alkaline to use on its own can be adjusted using white vinegar, while water that is too acidic can be adjusted using bicarbonate of soda. The pH of tap water may change with the seasons so a good idea is to test often. To find the right ratios for your situation start with a single gallon of untreated water and then add small amounts of adjuster until you figure out how much is required to adjust the pH by one point. After that, you can use some simple math to suit your situation. The time frame of each adjuster is different, and can be affected by how you apply them to your grow. Soil-based systems can take immediate advantage of water-diluted adjusters. Alternatively, additives can be mixed into the soil before planting for a more long-term effect. Acidic soils can be adjusted with lime powder. There are many types of lime available for growers to use; some act almost immediately while others may start working after a few months. This information is usually available on the packaging.

Gardeners can adjust alkaline soils by adding either aluminum sulfate or sulfur. Aluminum sulfate is the preferred adjuster, as it will change the soil pH instantly, because as soon as the aluminum dissolves into the soil it produces the desired acidic effect. Sulfur is used less commonly as it takes a long time for bacteria in the soil to convert it into sulfuric acid, meaning that it could take months before you see the change.

Because adjusters like lime and sulfur are really designed to alter large amounts of soil, such as a full yard, most indoor marijuana growers prefer to use water-based adjusters that act almost immediately and can be easily calculated for small-scale use.

Feeding Ratios and Schedules

This is particularly difficult to understand at first, so pay attention. If you're new to growing, use a standard fertilizer such as a 10-10-10 mix or 20-20-20 (with the numbers representing the relative amounts of N, P and K) and dilute it down to 1-1-1 or 3-3-3. Use this mix for the entire lifespan of the plants. This method works perfectly well for new growers, but if you build up some confidence in the process you can alter the ratios to 1-3-1 or 3-5-3 during the floral stage to increase bud growth. If you really want to excel, you can start manipulating the ratios for each individual stage of the plants' growth.

My general rule is as follows: seedlings and clones require a weaker vegetative formula (such as 1-1-1 or 3-3-3); mature vegetative growth requires a formula high

Lesson 1.3: *Nutrients*

Necrosis like this clearly signals a possible nutrient overdose and immediate steps must be taken to save the plant.

Suggested NPK Ratios

Relative amounts of nitrogen (N), phosphorus (P) and potassium (K):

Seedlings and Clones: 1-1-1 or 3-3-3
Mature Vegetative: 3-1-1 or 5-3-3
Flowering: 1-3-3 or 3-5-3

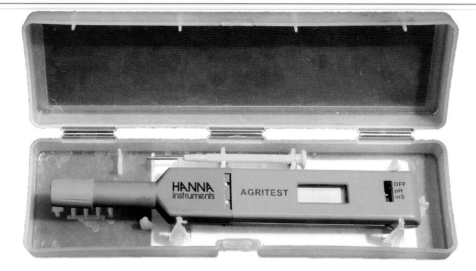

Monitoring and maintaining proper nutrient and pH levels is critical to success.

in nitrogen (such as 3-1-1 or 5-3-3); and flowering plants require a formula high in potassium and low in nitrogen (such as 1-3-3 or 3-5-3).

Rejuvenating plants use the same formula as the young seedlings. After two or three weeks of recovery growth switch to the stronger mature vegetative formulas.

It's hard to tell you exactly when you should fertilize your particular plants, as the fertilizer brand, its strength, medium type, water pH, and plant genetics all come into play. The main thing to remember is this: do not over do it. A little goes a long way, and if you give the plants too much they will overdose and, if left untreated, die. The nutrient overdose locks up the plant's ability to absorb water, so it dehydrates your marijuana. The plants may die in a few hours after receiving the fatal dose.

The most common signs that you've used too much fertilizer are extremely dark colored leaves and plant burn at the very tips of the leaves. The burn will be brown or gray and crumble between your fingers. If your plants show this sign, stop fertilizing!

If you're growing in a soil garden I don't suggest feeding the plants every time you water, even if the fertilizer instructions tell you to. Instead, feed them every second or third time you water. The nutrient-free watering will flush out any excess nutrients that could harm the plants.

Lesson 1.3: *Nutrients*

In a hydroponic system, the situation is different. The water usually has a weak nutrient formula in it at all times. To prevent overdosing, try using a mix that is only one-quarter strength. Every two or three weeks, drain the system and flush it out with nutrient-free water, then add water with fresh nutrients to the system. This will help control chemical buildup problems. My favorite hydroponic formulas are 1-1-1 and 0.5-0.5-0.5, as the low levels reduce the amount of buildup in hoses or pumps. Pre-mixed formulas with ratios like these are available at grow shops that cater to marijuana growers. Another approach is to fill the system with a full strength mix initially, then add nutrient-free water for a week or two. Drain the system, flush with clear water and start over.

For both soil and hydroponic gardens, when the time comes to flower the plants you should flush out the containers and/or system with lukewarm nutrient-free water to remove any excess nutrients. Afterwards, re-fertilize with a mixture that is low in nitrogen and high in phosphorus. The plants will still need some nitrogen so don't remove it completely.

A white buildup will appear on the surfaces of containers, mediums, drain trays, and basins. Don't be too concerned about this; it's chemical salts from the fertilizers and water. However, such salts will affect the nutrient and pH levels so be sure to scrub it off between crops.

Chapter Summary

Nitrogen (N), phosphorus (P)) and potassium (K) are the most important nutrients for marijuana plants. NPK testing kits are essential.

Chlorosis and necrosis can be symptoms of a serious nutrient deficiency.

There are a number of major and secondary nutrients that your plants always need.

Organic fertilizers are a viable alternative to chemical-based ones; do some research!

pH levels of both the water and medium can greatly affect your plants. Test pH levels often and use an appropriate adjuster if necessary.

Terms to Learn

- NPK
- Chlorosis
- Necrosis
- pH

Container Selection and Use

Unless you're growing outside, one of your initial concerns is going to be acquiring decent containers for your plants to live in. Store-bought pots can be expensive, so the smart grower knows where to look for substitutes. Milk cartons and drink cups make good starter containers for small plants, while one-gallon milk jugs with the tops removed are great medium-sized containers. Restaurants and deli shops throw away buckets of all sizes and shapes, so don't be afraid to ask for them. If you are growing in limited space, then stick to squared-off containers as they use garden space much more effectively than round ones.

Another option is to use grow bags, which are basically just round or square plastic bags with a flat bottom. When filled with medium they stand up straight, and work well in gardens where a lot of plants are grown together and can use each other for support. Some nurseries sell grow-bags of various sizes, so check out your local store.

It is important to remember that in soil-based gardens the size of the container affects the size of the plant; if you raise several plants in different size containers, the ones in the larger containers will produce more lush growth than their restricted counterparts. If a container is too small, the roots will be cramped, stunting the size of the whole plant. Marijuana grows very quickly, so plants that will be allowed to grow very large may have to be transferred several times before finishing. A simple guide to transferring is this: increase the container space by one gallon per month of growth up to six months, or the onset of flowering. The largest common container is five gallons. In hydroponic systems transferring the plants multiple times may be unnecessary, as many growers use smaller containers and allow the roots to grow out into the surrounding water reservoir.

Plant containers come in many sizes. The larger your plant, the bigger the container should be.

Requirements

Whatever containers you choose to use, make sure they are deep and wide enough to allow for proper root development. They also should be able to withstand repeated watering and physical abuse, which is why plastic containers are preferred. Proper water drainage is a must: you can't have too many drain holes, but you can have too few. If the containers trap water then the roots of your plants will drown.

Temporary Containers

Disposable containers are used once and then discarded. These are great for starting seedlings and clones. I liked to use sixteen-ounce plastic drink cups, while some growers prefer to use starter peat pots. These will decompose once transferred into a larger container filled with soil.

Recyclable Containers

If you're trying to be good to the environment, or keep the cost of growing down, consider reusable containers. The most common ones are made of plastic or terra cotta. Plastic nursery containers and buckets are lightweight, durable, and

Lesson 1.4: *Container Selection and Use*

non-porous, while terra cotta containers are more expensive, heavier, and break if handled roughly. Terra cotta is porous, meaning that you will have to place a plastic drop cloth under any terra cotta drain trays, otherwise water will pass through and leave a mark. They will also wear out quicker than plastic and have to be replaced sooner.

Preparing Containers

Be sure to wash any container thoroughly before using, even if it is brand new. If possible, run it through the dishwasher before planting.

If the containers don't have existing drainage holes then you will have to add them. If you're using paper and polystyrene cups you can do this with a pencil or pen, but for plastic drink cups it is better to use a small knife, ice pick, nail, or scissors to poke the holes. Be sure to round and smooth the edges of these holes to prevent root snagging.

An excellent young crop of OGA Seeds' Zombie Virus.

Growing Medium

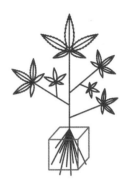

1-inch Rockwool or Rapid Rooter

1-inch Rockwool and 3-inch Rockwool

1-inch Rockwool or Rapid Rooter and Hydroton Stone

Step-by-step: Container Care

1. Prepare sterilizing tools.

2. Wash excess dirt off.

3. Measure the bleach and water.

4. Slowly add bleach to water.

5. Mix thoroughly.

6. Scrub pots.

7. Let pots air dry.

8. Rinse again with fresh water.

9. Your pot is ready!

Container Selection and Use

Checking for Root-Bound Plants

Plants become root bound when the roots have spread out through the entire medium, leaving no more space for growth. If they are left cramped, roots will begin to spiral around the walls of the container. In soil-based systems this is very bad, as the growth of the plants is then reduced and their general health may decline.

If you think a plant has become root bound, tap or massage the sides of the container to separate the root ball from the inside. If the root ball refuses to come loose, then run a butter knife around the inside walls of the container. If the whole mass of roots and medium comes out in one piece, and you can clearly see the vein work of the roots, this means that the plant is root bound. If the medium falls away and the root ball is still small and undeveloped, you'll simply have to wait longer.

Transferring Root-Bound Plants

For soil-based systems, first cover the drain holes with a coffee filter, single sheet of newspaper, or a piece of screen. Fill the bottom two inches of the containers with a good drain medium. The drain medium can be just about anything as long

Tip!

If a plant becomes root-bound, then the only cure is to transfer the plants into a larger container. As mentioned before, in most hydroponics systems the roots can be allowed to grow out into the surrounding water reservoir and therefore transferring may be unnecessary.

Be sure to scrub inside thoroughly.

Step-by-step: Transplanting

1. Fresh soil.

2. Rocks for drainage.

3. Water the soil.

4. Measure the depth.

5. Dig hole appropriately.

6. Remove root-bound plant.

7. Tease the roots out.

8. Plant in hole.

9. Pack in and water.

Lesson 1.4: Container Selection and Use

as it's inert and, of course, drains well. Pea gravel or small rocks are traditional, though perlite and polystyrene peanuts also work well.

Next, fill the new container about halfway with medium, then remove the root ball from its old container and inspect the root mass for any spiraling roots. If there are any, use a knife or your fingers to remove them. You should also score or gouge the sides of the root ball. It might seem a scary thing to do, but loosening the mass encourages the roots to spread out into the new medium faster. Place the root ball squarely on top of the new medium, and adjust its position until you can fill the container around the sides of the root ball with the new soil medium. Gently press down on the top of the medium to remove air pockets. Finally, give the plant a good watering. In fact, totally soak the medium. Like the gentle pressing this will help settle the medium and reduce transfer shock. Within a couple of weeks you should see a noticeable increase in your plant's health and vigor.

Chapter Summary

There are a variety of pots suitable for indoor growing, including terra cotta and plastic. Decide which will be best for your situation.

Your plant's container must be a sufficient size so as not to stunt growth or make the plant become root bound.

If your plants do become root bound, transferring them will be necessary.

Terms to Learn
- Root bound
- Hydroponic
- Root ball

Pests

All kinds of pests plague the marijuana grower, but most fall into one of three distinct categories: human, microbiological, or insect. By following simple security measures and keeping the garden clean most problems can be avoided.

Having said this, almost every grower eventually has the misfortune to encounter at least one pest problem, as pests may accidentally stumble into the garden or be brought in by the growers themselves. To avoid this, never visit your garden directly after working with houseplants or being outdoors.

Human

Humans come in many forms and are the most dangerous kind of predator in the cannabis jungle. Humans involved in law enforcement are the worst kind. Thieves, friends turned "narc," and blabber-mouths are unfortunately well-known to most growers, and the only real form of defense is to never tell anyone, not even your best friend or pet lizard, that you are growing. Keeping the air in your house odor-free with a good ventilation system, ion generators, and/or air deodorizers is also key.

Microbiological

The microbiological enemy is an invisible alliance of fungus, bacteria, mold, and viral armies. The worst time to develop a microbiological problem is during the flowering period, when the buds and colas of the plant are easily rotted. Disinfecting the garden area and supplies before using them is the first line of defense against these pests. Follow this action with other preventative measures, such as the use of a proper ventilation system that vigorously circulates and exchanges the garden air; this will keep spores and insects from settling in the garden. Good circulation of fresh air also cuts down on excessive humidity, which can be a serious problem.

Dead leaves and organic debris are a veritable breeding ground for fungus and mold. A few leaves cluttered in a corner or hanging from a lower branch could saturate a crop with spores and rot the buds before your very eyes. Remove debris

Fungus has invaded the entire stem.

This mold will spread if unchecked.

Botrytis destroying a hybrid.

as soon as you see it so it won't become a problem.

Viral infections can come from contaminated soil or manure fertilizers. Never reuse soils and mediums, and always sanitize containers between crops.

Insects

Warfare, survival instinct; call it what you will: insects are prepared to do everything to stay in your garden, and you will do anything to wipe them out. To escape this "stale mate" situation, start with an aggressive front line defense: prevent flying insects from gaining a foothold by installing a good ventilation system. Crawling insects are usually very hard to see until they begin doing severe damage to your plants, so use a magnifying glass to inspect the plants routinely, and deal with any infiltrators promptly.

Once established in your garden, it is nearly impossible to get pests out. All you can do is try to keep the numbers down, and in this endeavor, you have several options. The most common weapon is an insecticide spray. Farmers used chemicals for decades to try and protect our food sources, but seem to have damaged the Earth in the process. Today, many farmers and home gardeners have made the switch to organic pesticide alternatives, just as they have with their choice of medium. If you can, use a natural organic spray because it's safer for the plants, the environment, and your lungs. Organic sprays are very common and well stocked in garden supply shops. Always use sprays that are free of weed killer. More passive sprays simply contain liquid dishwasher soap that dries up the little pests. Horticultural sprays are very effective when used every ten days for a month.

You could try enlisting the help of mercenaries by releasing hoards of predator insects to hunt down and kill the pests for you. Common predator insects include ladybugs, praying mantises, predator mites, and others. You may have to release several waves of these predators to ensure that enough stay in the garden.

Common Insects
Mites

Mites are treated like insects, but in reality they are arachnids: eight-legged relatives of spiders. Mites live in big families upside down on the bottom sides of leaves, and they can be brown, red, or black in color.

Because mites are so tiny at little more than specks, you won't see them until they have already moved in. The most common sign of a mite infestation is the fine

Lesson 1.5: *Pests*

Deodorizers remove the smell of cannabis to deter nosy human predators.

webbing of silk they leave on plants. Another is a blemish on the topside of leaves, kind of like a scab, which is the result of the bugs sucking the liquid out of the leaves from the bottom.

Aphids

Aphids can appear on your plants thanks to the ants that farm them for the honeydew liquid they secrete. The honeydew residue encourages fungus on the plants.

Whiteflies

Whiteflies are moths about an eighth of an inch long, and as the name suggests

Common Insect Pests

Mites

White flies

Aphids

Fungus gnats

Termites

Step-by-step: Garlic Water Insecticide

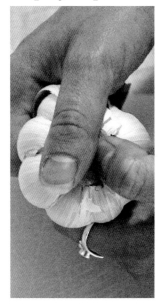
1. Skin some garlic.

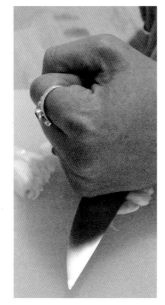
2. Mash the cloves.

3. Well-mashed garlic.

4. Boil water.

5. Steep garlic ten minutes.

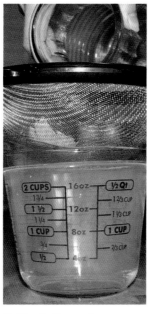
6. Strain the water.

7. Put in spray bottle.

8. Spray to deter insects.

Lesson 1.5: *Pests*

Step-by-step: Tobacco Water Insecticide

1. Take cigarette.

2. Remove the tobacco.

3. Place in tea filter.

4. Put in container.

5. Add boiling water.

6. Steep for five minutes.

7. Strain into spray bottle.

8. Spray to deter insects.

Step-by-step: Soap Water Insecticide

Mix two teaspoons of dish soap with one quart of water, mix thoroughly, and spray on plants. Leave it on the plants for twenty minutes and then rinse it off with clean water.

Tip!

A simple soap spray will dry up both aphids and mites. Follow up the soap sprays with plain water showers to remove excess soap and prevent leaf burn.

they are white in color. You will know if you have them, as disturbing a plant slightly will cause them to buzz around for a while. Whiteflies lay eggs that hatch larva. These larvae excrete a residue similar to that of the aphids, and like the aphid residue it can promote fungus. Some companies sell bright yellow cards covered with a sticky substance, which attract and trap the flies; place these in your garden before you get a problem and they may just catch that lusty couple before they have a chance to start a happy little family in your plants. If that doesn't work, and they move the kids in anyway, a vacuum cleaner with a flexible hose attachment can be used to suck up the whiteflies one at a time. Simply shake on the plants one by one and snag them as they buzz around. This is also a preferable option when the plants are flowering and sprays may pollute the buds.

Fungus Gnats

Gnats look just like miniature houseflies, and I've had a lot of experience with these little devils. In the early days I had a small closet soil-based garden. The gnats flew in through a hole in my window screen. They were attracted to the soil and burrowed down into it. At first there were one or two, then dozens, then too many to count.

Whenever I watered or otherwise disturbed my crop, swarms of gnats would buzz in my face. I was halfway through a crop and couldn't start over so I got some sticky cards in the garden. I also increased the air circulation with some additional fans. I can still remember many stoned hours sitting in front of my garden hunting and swatting the gnats among the leaves and branches of my beauties.

Other Pests

Mice, termites, and ants may also affect your grow, and even deer can become a problem if plants are planted or moved outdoors.

To remove mice simply use baits or traps to kill them, or catch them so they can be released outdoors. If you let them go, look for the way they got in and seal it off, otherwise they'll be back. Ant and termite traps (motels) or chemical barriers are effective and readily available. Keeping your place clean and crumb-free also helps prevent ants. Preventing infestations stops the neighbors from hiring exterminators who will more than likely discover that you and your highly illegal plants are the source of the problem—a situation you definitely want to avoid.

Cutting up a few bars of soap and spreading the pieces around the perimeter of the garden as well as spraying predator urine around the area can repeal deer, as they don't like either smell. Hopefully you won't ever encounter this problem indoors, but if you do then you have some serious security problems to address before you continue gardening. I would also skip the urine part, as it gets a bit intense in enclosed spaces.

Chapter Summary

Human pests can often be the most devastating kind; never forget that your grow is in danger at all times.

Dead leaves and debris can harbor mold and fungus, so dispose of them immediately.

Good ventilation is important in order to minimize insect problems.

Predator insects can be preferable to chemical sprays, and just as effective.

Terms to Learn
- Predator insects
- Mites, aphids, white flies, and fungus gnats
- Fungus and bud rot
- Natural organic insecticides

The Atmosphere

People tend to forget about the essential things in life until they lose them: no one really appreciates how necessary it is to breathe until they're choking in some restaurant, and the waiter is frantically reading the C.P.R. chart in the kitchen. If we don't breathe, we don't live, and plants are just the same. However, humans and other animals inhale oxygen and exhale carbon dioxide (CO_2), while plants do the opposite. This is why we live so well together. For this reason, providing your garden with the proper atmosphere should be given as much attention as any other aspect of growing, if not more. You want your plants to live, after all.

Ventilation

When we talk about ventilation in horticulture, we're talking about the exchange of air into and out of the garden as well as the movement of air inside the room. There are two forms of indoor garden ventilation: passive and active.

Passive ventilation is achieved via an open door or window that allows the air to just drift in and out of the garden as it would in any other room. This is the easiest method of ventilating your grow room, but can lead to problems like excessive humidity and temperature buildup that will quickly stress the plants and limit their growth. Also, an open door or window greatly increases the possibility of the garden being discovered.

An **active ventilation** system is created by using fans and/or connected ducts to exchange the garden's air. You can use small desk fans or larger ones, depending on the size of your grow room, placed around the room in a way that promotes a continuous flow of fresh air. By doing this many factors like smell, heat and humidity will be controlled. Situate intake fans low down, to bring cool air into the lower areas of the garden, and the exhaust near the ceiling to efficiently remove any heat build up.

Circulation

To create sufficient circulation, the air inside your garden needs to be moving all the time. This will dramatically reduce problems with heat, humidity, and fungi, and

Fix!

Fix a humid grow area by increasing your ventilation and/or circulation, or, if necessary, by placing a dehumidifier in the garden. Installing covers over the tops of basins and reservoirs will also help a lot.

Let in a fresh breeze or create your own.

may even prevent them entirely if you're lucky. Proper circulation should be strong enough to gently sway the plants; if the leaves are moving, you've got the right idea. This will strengthen the plants' branches, and having stronger branches means that they can support larger buds. Think of it as exercise for the plants.

Humidity

Humidity refers to the amount of moisture in the air. A high level of humidity encourages mold and fungi. Plants excrete water, much like we do whenever we sweat, so grow rooms can become overly humid. Hydroponics systems in particular will greatly raise the humidity of a garden, especially when hot lights are used. Soil-based gardens may experience increased humidity levels just after watering.

Temperature

Plants are happiest in an area of moderate heat: around seventy to eighty degrees Fahrenheit. If it is too hot or cold their growth may be hindered. The natural

Aim fans above plants or bounce air off of walls. Never aim directly at plants!

temperature of your garden depends on its location: non-insulated attics have the biggest problems with temperature fluctuation, while stuffy closets and small rooms allow heat to build up quickly. A basement may have a cold floor but the atmosphere will usually be more insulated, so elevate the bottoms of plant containers from the floor to keep them from getting chilled.

Wherever your garden is located, proper ventilation and circulation will fix most heat buildup problems. If you have the opposite problem and it's too cold, try installing a heater with a temperature gauge. When the temperature drops the heater should kick in and keep the plants warm all night.

Odor

The smell of your garden won't affect the plants, but it might affect their security. Strong odors can give away even the most carefully concealed garden, so it is in your best interests to get rid them.

The best means of removing smell is with a good ventilation system like the

Warning!

Law enforcement sometimes uses thermal imaging cameras to look for hot walls that could mean a grow operation is going on. Be smart and prevent heat buildup.

Tip!

Because HIDs generate a lot of heat, growers who use these will want to pay special attention to ventilation.

Keep your garden neat and tidy to prevent accidents and claustrophobia.

ones outlined above. Beyond that, ion generators, air deodorizers, and charcoal filters are the most effective devices for removing or masking the smell of a garden full of skunk. To gain the best results deploy ion generators and/or deodorizers in both the garden and any adjoining rooms.

Ion generators produce negative ions that physically neutralize the odor molecules. The cleansed air smells very pleasant, like a waterfall or the air after rain. Generators come in various sizes and models. In a small garden you may have to use several of the smaller models, while larger gardens may require high flow models that act more like ion cannons.

Deodorizers simply mask the odor using a scent. An automatic device can be utilized to release a spray of scent every 15 minutes or so, similar to the ones

Lesson 1.6: *The Atmosphere*

Step-by-step: Build Your Own Carbon Air Filter

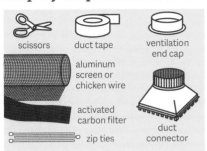

1. What you need to get started.

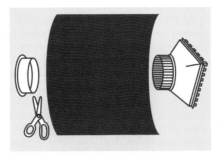

2. End cap and connector piece separated by activated carbon filter blanket. Blanket is being cut to size.

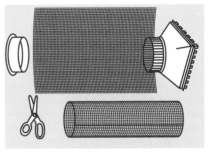

3. Make a tube out of the aluminum screen that goes between the end-cap and connector piece.

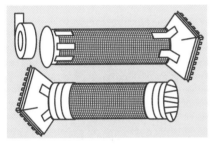

4. Fasten the three pieces together: the chicken wire tube runs from the end cap to the connector piece.

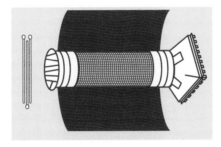

5. Wrap the activated carbon filter blanket around the chicken wire, and fasten with the zip ties.

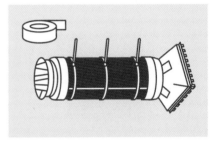

6. Add duct tape to make sure air doesn't escape around the edges of the activated carbon blanket.

7. Attach to the exhaust outlet of your grow room's ventilation system.

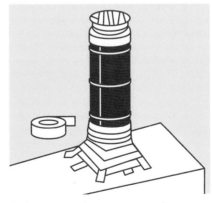

8. Duct tape the connector piece to the exhaust system.

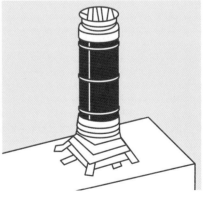

9. Filter attached to exhaust system, no more smells!

Danger!

Negative ion generators can affect computers and fluorescent lamps so give them some distance. They also attract dust and require routine cleaning and/or filter changing.

Carbon Dioxide

Some growers use CO_2 to increase the growth rate of their cannabis plants. Personally, I feel that it should be used during the vegetative cycle, to decrease the overall growing time, and discontinued during the floral period.

Tip!

Concentrate on learning the basics of growing before tackling the more expert aspects.

you might find around your house. Others have a small fan mounted over an open container of liquid air freshener; I used one of these for several years before the fan broke. It also won't hurt to fill your place with the kind of air fresheners that plug into electrical sockets.

Charcoal filters can be installed in ventilation systems to remove the odor before it's released outside the garden. Charcoal filters are very effective at removing smell, and are highly recommended for whenever air is expelled outside at ground level.

CO_2

Plants use CO_2, along with water and light, to make their food through the process of photosynthesis. Normally, air contains about .03 to .04 percent CO_2. If the level is increased to .15 percent the growth rate of the plant, between sprouting and maturation, speeds up dramatically. Some growers believe that using CO_2 during the flower cycle will even increase the mass of the floral growth. Personally, I feel that it should be used during the vegetative cycle, to decrease the overall growing time, and discontinued during the floral period. CO_2 enriched buds seem much leafier to me.

Small, passively ventilated gardens such as stuffy closets could benefit from a slow constant flow of CO_2 during the light cycle, because plants can tolerate heat stress better in a CO_2 enriched environment. In a garden with an active ventilation system, release the CO_2 while the exhaust fans are turned off, otherwise it will be pumped out of the garden before the plants have a chance to use it. As soon as the exhaust fans turn off, quickly saturate the garden and then give the plants enough time to use the gas before you allow the fans to pump out the used air.

During the dark cycle plants don't carry out the process of photosynthesis, so any CO_2 being released into the garden during the dark cycle is wasted. A smart grower will discontinue CO_2 production while the plants sleep.

There are several ways to introduce more CO_2 into your grow room safely.

Generators and Tanks

CO_2 Generators

Generators burn natural gas, or, preferably, propane gas, to produce CO_2. I prefer generators that use propane, as it is easier to have refilled than natural gas; so many people use this gas to barbecue that people assume you're going to be flipping burgers rather than raising weed, so buying it doesn't create suspicion.

Carbon dioxide can encourage faster growth and produce lush vegetative plants in a very short period of time.

Maintain the atmosphere of your entire grow room by using a good environmental controller.

Natural gas and propane are both compressed and quite flammable, and leaks could result in asphyxiation or an explosion. Use extreme caution when employing them.

CO_2 Tanks

I don't recommend experimenting with CO_2 tanks if you are a beginner grower. They are expensive to buy and require some expertise to set up and refill. They can also be dangerous because if they are damaged there is a risk that they may become unguided missiles. If you have a proper ventilation system, then I don't suggest installing a CO_2 system.

The grow room at Alpine Seeds needs a huge air filter to handle the scent of all those dank buds.

Lesson 1.6: *The Atmosphere*

Saturate gardens by releasing carbon dioxide over the tops of plants or near circulation fans.

The Math, or, "How Much Gas Per Cubic Foot?"

In a CO_2 tank each pound equals about 8.5 cubic feet of gas, so a 20-pound tank contains roughly 170 cubic feet of gas. To saturate a garden you must release .15 feet^3 of gas for every 100 cubic feet. For example, let's say you're using a closet 6 feet deep, 5 feet wide, and 7 feet tall; a total of 210 cubic feet. To properly saturate this garden you would have to release roughly .30 feet^3 of gas. If you are running your lights 24 hours a day and you saturate the garden 10 times a day you would be using 3.0 feet^3 worth of gas every day. So, a 20-pound tank would last you roughly 56 days. In the same size garden with poor ventilation, a constant flow of CO_2 running at a rate of .25 feet^3 per hour would use 6.0 pounds a day. A 20-pound tank would then last the grower about 28 days.

Chapter Summary

Though a passive ventilation system can be sufficient, consider an active one to control smell, heat and humidity properly.

Air inside the grow room should be constantly moving.

Plants are most comfortable at seventy to eighty degrees Fahrenheit, so keep your room between these temperatures.

Additional CO2 can be introduced to a grow room via generators or tanks, with the goal of increasing the mass of floral growth.

Terms to learn
- Passive ventilation
- Active ventilation

Light

After security, the most important thing you can spend your money on is lighting. Light is the heart of the garden, and the amount of light used is the strongest factor in determining how large and productive the garden will be. Finding the right light source is the main hurdle to actually growing any plant, especially weed. Take your time to look around for the best window or set of electric lights.

Growers can use light to control almost every aspect of plant development. An informed grower can manipulate growth rates, trigger flowering, and sometimes for even force a female plant to become a hermaphrodite for breeding purposes. The most important things to understand are light cycles, intensity and the spectrum.

The phrase "light cycle" means how many hours of light and darkness the plants are exposed to during a 24-hour period. The amount of light the plants are exposed to will determine how fast a plant will grow and whether it will produce vegetative or floral growth.

The term "intensity" refers to the strength of the light. The intensity of electric lamps varies with the wattage of the lamp and the distance between the lamp and the plants.

You may already know that the spectrum basically refers to the color, or wavelengths, of the light. You might not know that marijuana plants prefer specific wavelengths of the spectrum. The two most important are blue and red. The only color the plants don't use is green, which they reflect. This reflected light is what makes the plants appear green to our eyes.

The Light Cycle

Like it or not, if you want to grow big buds you're going to have to concentrate for a few moments and memorize some big numbers. Don't worry too much; it will be over soon, and we won't get into advanced algebra.

As I mentioned before, how much light a plant is exposed to during a 24-hour

A good light timer is invaluable as a grow accessory. Unlike a human, a light timer will never forget to turn the lights on or off during the plant's growth cycle.

period directly affects how fast a plant grows and what type of growth a plant will produce. Plants exposed to lots of light, such as twenty-four hours a day, will grow quickly and produce vegetative (non-floral) growth. Plants exposed to shorter light cycles of 12 hours a day or less will produce floral growth. Plants exposed to very short light cycles, like eight hours a day, may change sex.

Controlling vegetative growth is relatively simple. Expose the plants to the longest light cycles and they grow as quickly as they can. Every hour you chip off will slow the plants down.

Growers use long light cycles to raise young plants like seedlings and clones. As the plants get older they may threaten to outgrow their garden space. This is where reducing the light cycle can come in handy.

Controlling floral growth is a little bit trickier. In order to force plants to flower, the grower must expose them to steady periods of 12-hour darkness. After about two weeks of exposure to this dark cycle, the plants should begin to flower.

During the floral growth stage plants are fickle and unforgiving to error. During the actual dark period, the plants produce a chemical called phytochrome. When enough phytochrome is produced—for instance when they're exposed to 12 hours of darkness—the plant believes it's Fall and therefore time to flower. Phytochrome is photosensitive and is instantly destroyed by exposure to light. Even a brief flash of light is enough to ruin an entire night's supply. Light pollution during the flowering stage may prevent the plants from flowering, or even worse, produce hermaphrodite flowers. Some stubborn strains, mainly Sativa ones, may take a really long time to finish flowering. Some growers will cut the cycle down to one that gives only 11 hours of light to 13 hours of darkness in order to speed up the maturation process. The only downside to this method is that the plants will produce smaller buds.

Common Vegetative Cycles

24/7 light cycle: The fastest growth will occur.

18 on 6 off: The plants growth is reduced by roughly 30 percent.

16 on 8 off: This is the shortest vegetative cycle recommended; it should reduce the growth rate by 40 to 50 percent.

Long Light Floral Cycles

A fairly recent theory is that once the plants begin to flower, a multiple day timer can be used to expose the plants to long light flowering cycles that don't adhere to a twenty-four-hour template, such as 24 on/12 off or 18 on/12 off. Multiple day timers are commonly used to run landscaping lights and sprinkler systems over the course of a week or longer. They may cost more to buy and usually require some electrical wiring, so if you don't have any electrician experience, stick to the twenty-four-hour models used to run the standard 12 on/12 off cycle. We don't want you to burn your house down. However, if you think you know what you're

Under fluorescents keep the lights no more than a couple of inches above the plant tops.

doing (and aren't kidding yourself about your abilities) then try them out. Spending less time waiting for your harvest will make a hundred dollars seem like a small amount to spend on a timer.

As long as the plants continue to receive steady 12-hour periods of darkness they will produce floral growth, regardless of the length of their fake "days." The difference is that they now have longer periods of light in which to actually grow. By extending the grow time during flowering, a grower can reduce the overall flowering process by weeks. It is estimated that the 24 on/12 off cycle will cut three weeks or more off, while the 18 on/12 off cycle will knock about two weeks off. With a small grow, running a cycle like 30 on/12 off won't produce enough buds to justify the electric bill.

Saving Electricity Through Light Cycles

Reducing the light cycle does more than just slow plant growth rates down or force them to flower: it can also save you some money. A 700-watt garden costs between forty and a hundred dollars a month, depending on where you live, and a 1,300-watt garden can easily run over one or two hundred dollars a month. By turning the lights and other equipment off for a few hours a day you can save

Common Floral Cycles

13 on 11 off: Some indica strains will flower under this cycle.

12 on 12 off: The traditional flowering cycle is always good.

11 on 13 off: This short flowering cycle will make the plants finish flowering sooner, but the buds will be smaller.

Recommended Light Source Garden Space Ratios

Lamp type	Grow Area	Total
Four 4-foot fluorescent 160 watts	2 x 4 feet	8 feet^2
Four 8-foot fluorescent 320 watts	2 x 8 feet	16 feet^2
HID 175 watts	2 x 2 feet	4 feet^2
HID 400 watts	4 x 4 feet	16 feet^2
HID 1,000 watts	6 x 6 feet	36 feet^2
HID 2,000 watts	10 x 10 feet	100 feet^2

A very nice grow room with OGA Seeds strains. Good lighting and great genetics.

yourself a good chunk of change. Another benefit is that by turning the lights off you give them a rest period that saves on equipment wear and tear.

Natural Light

Natural light is the first source most beginners use to grow plants. I grew my first successful plants in an upstairs window, although skylights, balconies, and back porches also work well. Sunlight is obviously very strong and can produce fast, heavy growth from the top of the plant to the bottom. It also has a complete balanced spectrum that provides all the wavelengths of light the plants needs. The length of sunlight provided every day of course depends on the season. During the summer the days are long and the plants produce vegetative growth. During the fall the days are shorter and the plants are forced to flower.

There are several negatives to using natural light. The first is that to use

Lesson 1.7: *Light*

Reflective screens redirect light back towards plants.

Warning!

Some law agencies have used paper trails to carry out sting operations that put a lot of people in jail. Be careful how you pay for your equipment and don't order grow supplies to your grow site. Furthermore, keep an eye on your electricity bill – sharp increases in usage can make people suspicious.

sunlight the plants must somehow be exposed to the outside world. Security is a big issue; in this situation, anyone passing by such as a cop, dope thief, noisy neighbors, or even the local news helicopter may spot them. Venetian blinds turned to let light in and eyes out work very well, and some growers use an opaque material to cover windows or skylights. The best are white curtains or white Plexiglas roofing sheets. Place such materials on the room side of blinds so they're not noticed from the outside.

Secondly, the sun moves across the sky during the day and it's difficult to find a window that receives enough strong light to support all the plant's needs. In the northern hemisphere, windows that face south receive the most direct and abundant sunlight. In the southern hemisphere the opposite is true.

Finally, the sun's intensity and light schedule changes from season to season. Natural light growers traditionally start plants in the spring or early summer and

Light Fixtures and Accessories

HID Ballast.

Quantum T5 Lamps.

Badboy T5 Fluorescent Lighting.

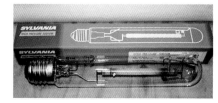

HPS Bulb.

Mothership LED from GrowL LED.

600 Watt Metal Halide Bulb.

75 Watt Neutral from GrowL LED.

HID Light with Vent.

Bulb with Reflector Hood.

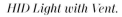

Shepherd bulb from GrowL LED.

Lesson 1.7: *Light*

harvest them in late summer or fall. Indoor growers can use simple electric lamps to extend short days and thick curtains to shorten long days. With these simple additions, an indoor grower can complement and manipulate the growth of their plants during any season, but an outdoor grower cannot.

Electric Light

When shopping for a lamp, the main things to look for are the wattage and the shade of the spectrum. The wattage refers to how strong or intense the light source is, and the spectrum refers to the color of the light given off.

Electric lights vary greatly in intensity and spectrum depending on the model and wattage. A simple electric timer must be used to control the timing cycle. Never try to control light cycles manually as the plants need a steady rhythmic cycle that's near impossible to create yourself. Humans, especially stoned ones, have a tendency to forget important things like turning the grow room lights off every day at 5:30.

When buying light bulbs and tubes you'll see the wattage listed on either the bulb itself or the packaging. To grow anything at all, you will need at least twenty watts of light per square foot of growth. To grow really great buds you should use thirty to forty watts of light for every square foot of growth.

Working out how much wattage you need is very simple. Take the size of the area you are using to grow in square feet and multiply it by twenty. For example, if your garden space is four feet by four feet, a total of sixteen square feet, multiply 16 by 20. For this grow, 320 watts would be the minimum you need to foster worthwhile growth. To enhance growth, and if you don't mind spending a little more on the electricity bill, you can multiply the size of the grow space by thirty or forty and use that figure as your guide.

Common Electric Lamps

For most amateurs, cruising the local DIY hardware store for a good grow light can be a very daunting task. Unless you know exactly what you're looking for, walking through the light department is enough to make your brain hurt. There are a million and one lights and lamp fixtures in this world and only a few are right for growing pot.

Incandescent lights are the common light bulbs that screw into standard table lamps. They do not foster growth, but do come in handy for extending a light cycle or intensifying the light along a garden border. They're also helpful when you

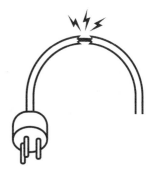

Danger!

Check cords often for excessive heat, nicks, or exposed wire. Weed is great but don't burn down your house because of a ten-foot strip of wire and plastic.

Fluorescents can conform to odd spaces which help make gardens as flexible as the grower's imagination.

can't use the main light in a garden, for example if you're doing some maintenance or misting your plants with water. Other lights suitable for additional lighting are halogen bulbs, spotlights, and circle or standard fluorescents.

Fluorescents are the tube lights you see in schools and grocery stores. They come in a variety of lengths, wattages, and spectrums. For a beginner, fluorescents are excellent as they are a cheap and effective light source to experiment with.

High Intensity Discharge lamps, (HIDs) are the powerful lights used to illuminate parking lots and ball games. They are efficient lamps to use for maturing crops. Using a 400- or 1,000-watt lamp, a grower can harvest between four ounces and a pound of weed. The two most common types of HIDs are metal halides (MH) and high-pressure sodium (HPS).

Lesson 1.7: *Light*

A smart grower will use fluorescent lights to sprout and root seedlings, and then switch to or add a HID to the garden to finish the plants. Very young plants don't like the heat generated by HIDs and will burn easily. A small, cool-running fluorescent system can foster healthy growth in dozens of young plants for the first three to four weeks. Fluorescent lights also use less electricity than HIDs, reducing your electric bills. However, once the plants are past the delicate seedling stage they will crave stronger light.

Fluorescents

My first electrical garden used only four four-foot fluorescent tubes; a total of 160 watts. With good plants I grew a couple of ounces of decent stuff in a few months.

Fluorescents have many advantages that ensure they will always have a place in the modern marijuana grower's gardens. Besides being cheap and readily available, they also have a very low running cost, and can conform to odd spaces like under stairs or along vertical walls. Fluorescents can be hung at an angle to light plants of different heights or stages of development. Pitiful harvests are usually the result of incorrect distancing between the lights and the tops of the plants. The light emitted by fluorescents is spread out along the length of the tubes. This results in the intensity of the light weakening dramatically as the distance between the light and plants increases. The drop off is so sharp that the prime buddage zone is less than a foot below the tubes. Always keep the tops of the plants within one to three inches below the tubes at all times, but no closer.

Another limitation of fluorescents is that the light emitted at the ends of the tubes is weaker than the center. Plants should either be placed about six inches from the ends, or rotated every day or two to ensure they maintain an even growth.

A third disadvantage with fluorescents is that they dim over time. To grow the best plants replace tubes often, at least once a year. I liked to replace mine with every crop. Save old tubes for rooting clones or supporting mother plants.

Specifics on Fluorescent Tubes

You may have come across fluorescents that are advertised as "Grow Lights." These tubes are coated to provide richer levels of blue and red light. According to the manufacturers, these tubes provide maximum results, and last for around two to three years. They cost ten to twenty dollars apiece. Are they worth it? In my opinion, they are not, as simple cool white tubes put out more light.

Danger!

Because HIDs are so powerful they can become very hot. Always use extreme caution when watering or misting the plants because even a single micro-drop of water could cause the bulb to explode. Pot is great but is it worth answering all those cop questions while the doctor flushes the shards of glass out of your eyes? The best preventative measure is to turn the lights off and let them cool for thirty minutes before working around them.

Danger!

Never try to construct a lamp from scratch unless you have professional electrical training. Jury-rigged lamps are dangerous to be around and could possibly start a fire.

Different types of fluorescents radiate different types of spectrums; some are more blue and some more red. A grower can tailor the spectrum for the different stages of plant growth; more blue for vegetative growth and more red for floral growth. In my opinion, however, manipulating the spectrum with fluorescents isn't a necessity. Cool model or standard shop lights provide a balanced spectrum capable of raising plants from start to finish.

Tubes rated as high output (HO) and very high output (VHO) give off more light than regular tubes. They also use slightly more electricity and can be hard to find because they are a specialty item.

High Intensity Discharge Lamps

HIDs lamps are the lights used to illuminate parking lots and sporting coliseums. Because the light is radiated from a point, it is more intense than that given off by fluorescents. It will also penetrate deeper into plant foliage, producing heavier yields. HID bulbs are good for around two or three years and cost between twenty and fifty dollars each, depending on wattage and type. A lot of growers replace their bulbs every year just to be more productive.

Daisy chained HID lamps can make gardens like this possible.

Lesson 1.7: *Light*

A single HID lamp on a light rail would have cut this garden's electric bill in half, but more lights mean more buds!

Buying an HID

HIDs can be difficult to come by. If you live in an area that has a good head shop or nursery carrying grow lamps, you should be able to find one that doesn't require any serious assembly. If there aren't any shops in your immediate area you may want to make a road trip to another city or state. It will be well worth the journey.

The next best place to go for a lamp is the local hardware store. Go to a large one when it's busy, so the employees don't have time to ask you too many awkward questions. A good excuse for buying a light is that you want to illuminate your driveway so you can play a little basketball at night. The box will list a million and one uses on the side, so pick one of them. These lamps may require some assembly.

Garden magazines carry ads for grow lights and other gardening equipment. I don't suggest this measure, but if you are stupid enough to order one from these sources never ship a grow lamp to the same place you will be growing. Always use cash or money orders to pay for a light. Never use anything that leaves a paper trail, like checks or credit cards.

Ballasts

Ballasts are power sources specifically designed to run electrical lamps. They are very specific about the models they will run. Never try to run an MH bulb on HPS ballast or vice versa. Ballasts range in price from sixty to two hundred dollars. Grow stores carry the best models in which the fixture, bulb, socket, and ballast are sold as a unit. The ballast is separated from the socket and fixture by a long electrical cord, thus reducing the weight of the fixture dramatically.

Always keep the ballast in a secure, safe, ventilated area free of any clutter. Place it out of the way on a closet shelf, supported by bricks or placed outside the garden chamber. The idea is to prevent any water from the garden getting on the ballast. It could short out and give you a dangerous shock.

The HID Reflector

Reflectors direct light in a controlled manner. Lamps without reflectors are highly inefficient, and any time I see plants under a naked bulb I feel sorry for them and their ill-informed grower. All that wasted light being thrown around could be used to make bigger, fatter buds.

There are three basic models of HID reflector for the pot grower: the horizontal, the vertical, and the box.

Horizontal reflectors are my favorite. They make better use of light than any other reflectors because the bulb is mounted horizontally, directing more of its surface area directly towards the plants.

Vertical reflectors mount the bulb vertically so most of the light is initially aimed sideways and has to be redirected by the reflector. Vertical reflectors mix spectrums very well when two or more lamps are used.

Box reflectors come with most hardware and are normally DIY models. They are generally smaller and may be very heavy and bulky, making them difficult to mount. Using a simple homemade reflector may be a better option, as they can easily be made out of sturdy cardboard painted flat white. Such a reflector can be attached to the outside of the existing fixture without much difficulty.

Certain lamps (100–250 watts) should always be mounted horizontally, as they need all the help they can get. The mid- to high-powered lamps (400–1,500 watts) can be mounted either horizontally or vertically.

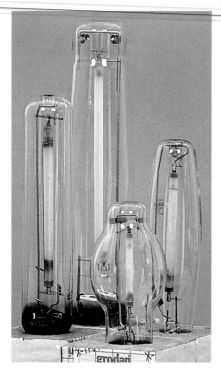

Most lamps and bulbs are not interchangeable. Always buy the corresponding wattage and correct style bulb for your lamp!

Lesson 1.7: *Light*

Danger!

LEDs are considered by some to be the future of indoor growing. However, as with all lights, you need to be sure that no heat or light signatures escape from your grow room. A police officer may be suspicious if it looks like an extra-terrestrial is living in your basement...

LED lamps are the latest craze for bud lamps.

A nice garden set up with a screen of green under LED lights by Growl LED.

High Pressure Sodium Lamps

HPS lamps cost more to buy than other lamps, but they use electricity in a more economical manner, so they pay for themselves over time. Also, many growers argue that they promote faster floral growth than the MH models.

Spectrum

Standard HPS bulbs give off a spectrum rich in red, orange, and yellow. These lamps work best for mature vegetative and flowering plants but are poor light sources for young vegetative plants, seedlings, and rooting clones. The enriched red spectrum will cause elongation of the stems, and the plants will develop problems later on in life. Grow stores sell newer bulbs that give off a more balanced spectrum suited for plants of all ages.

Garden Size to Wattage Ratios

Garden size in square feet	Lamp wattage and style
1-15	14-watt panel
	15-watt spotlight
5	45-watt panel
12	90-watt panel any style
50	300-watt panel any style
100	600-watt panel any style

The garden is illuminated by a gorgeous purple hue under these LED lights.

Metal Halides

Spectrum

MH lamps emit a bluish white light, which is good for use as a single light source. Some growers claim that because of their blue rich spectrum, MH lamps produce smaller buds than HPS lamps, but this is entirely a matter of opinion.

If I was raising some young plants not yet ready for a couple thousand watts of HIDs, I might use a mid-range MH to prepare them. After all, it would be a shame to run up a high electrical bill when you don't have to, and possibly burn your delicate plants.

Light Emitting Diodes

Light Emitting Diode (LED) lamps may be the new kid on the block in the growing world but Oleg Vladimirovich Losev created the first one back in the 1920s. Today,

Alpine Seeds grow room with reflective wall material.

OGA Seeds grow room with powerful lights.

NASA uses them in space to grow all kinds of plants; think about that the next time you get all red eyed and philosophical. LEDs have allowed a technological leap in indoor growing, similar to when indoor growers made the switch from fluorescents to HIDs back in the 1980s. I am confident that in the very near future they will become the de facto lighting system for the clandestine grower.

LEDs have several advantages over traditional HID and fluorescent lamps, the most attractive of which is the money factor. Though the initial cost of purchasing a good quality LED setup can be significantly more than buying the same quality of HID system, after that the savings start to add up very quickly. For example, a 90-watt LED system can illuminate a five- square-foot garden as well as a 400-watt HID lamp at about a quarter of the running expense. LEDs also produce very little heat, reducing the necessity of installing and running an expensive heat ventilation system. Growers may find that the cooling needs of most small- to moderate-sized gardens can instead be met by an aggressive air circulation system.

Additional savings are found in the low maintenance requirements of an LED

Danger!

Sodium explodes on contact with water. One should always use caution when working around hot bulbs with water. If a bulb breaks, don't pick up the pieces with your bare hands. Your sweat could cause the sodium to burn you. Likewise, use caution when disposing of an old bulb.

Lesson 1.7: *Light*

system. Standard fluorescents can begin to dim after a couple of crops, and a good HPS bulb may last less than 20,000 hours before you need to replace it. Running HID lamps also requires eventual replacement of the expensive ballast. The bulbs in a LED lamp, however, can last for 50,000 hours or more before they need to be replaced; when this happens, growers may find it cheaper to replace the whole lamp rather than to replace all the individual bulbs. If you happen to be environmentally-conscious it will make your green fingers tingle to learn that besides being thrifty with the electricity, LEDs don't contain harsh elements like mercury or sodium that can hurt the environment.

Another major advantage LEDs offer is an increase in security. Less heat and lower electrical bills means reduced visibility on law enforcement radars. Agents have been known to use thermal imaging technology to find gardens from the heat signature emitted by a room full of hot lamps and equipment. Even worse, electrical companies may report a sudden increase in electrical usage to the authorities, leading to your front door getting kicked in. A cooler and cheaper garden is a safer garden.

LEDs designed for growing are extremely efficient because they emit light waves between roughly 300 and 700 nanometers. This is basically the visible part of the light spectrum, and plants can absorb almost a hundred percent of it for photosynthesis. Other lighting systems waste a lot of power producing ultra-violet and infrared light waves that are unusable and even harmful to plants and people alike.

When they see a LED lamp working for the first time what most people notice right away is the monotone color scheme. Many of the lamps engulf the plants in a rich blue, red, or purple light that seems like it belongs on the set of a bad sci-fi movie. This is just one of the many things that sets LEDs apart from other lamps, but one gets used to it very quickly. Some growers switch between all blue lights for vegetative growing and all red for floral, while others decide to use a combination of red and blue bulbs that meet the needs of the plants for their entire life cycle.

Picking the right LED lamp for your garden is a little different from picking out other lights. The problem is that they use so little power that the usual math goes out the window. Instead of trying to cram another formula down your throat, I've put together a table of suggested wattages for the more common gardens sizes.

Of course, these are suggested listings for single lamps; using more than one lamp is rarely a bad idea. Several lower-wattage lamps in a small garden can bathe plants in light from all directions, and a couple of 300-watt mid-range lamps will cast a more even light over a moderate sea of green than a single higher-powered

Even a small closet can become a productive garden given the right imagination and equipment. Take note of the reflective sheeting and air circulation system.

Danger!

Metal Halides have a protective coating on the bulb. Normally when damaged the bulb will stop working, but if the damage is small enough the bulb may continue to function while emitting dangerous levels of ultra-violet radiation. This can cause permanent eye or skin damage. It's a good idea to use sunglasses, or special safety glasses that have a ultra-violet protective coating, whenever you are working around these lamps.

600-watt lamp would. Some growers have even been known to surround gardens with LED panels instead of using reflective materials like foil or flat white paint.

When figuring out the distance between the lights and the plants, keep in mind that the penetrating power of LEDs is somewhere between fluorescents and HIDs, meaning that you should keep them as close to the tops of the plants as possible. It helps if the lights are mounted on a movable system that can move the lamps accordingly to keep up with plant growth.

LEDs may take some getting used to, but they are so versatile and user-friendly that I have no doubt that you will be very happy with the results.

Mixing Spectrums

To produce a more natural spectrum some growers combine MH and HPS lamps. This is best done on a whirligig or another kind of light mover. The most common mix is one MH and one HPS lamp, but those who can afford it combine two MHs and one HPS lamps during vegetative growth and one MH with two HPSs during flowering. Of course, you can use more than just three lamps, but be prepared for the initial purchasing cost and the high electric bill. A sudden spike in electrical usage can be quite suspicious. Some electrical companies may come out to investigate it or simply tip off the police. I liked to use a couple of fluorescent lamps to balance out the spectrum of my mid-range HPS lamp. The plants loved it and I loved the reasonable electrical cost.

Light Improvements and Other Garden Extras

Electric gardens are costing you money for every second they operate; why not get the most bud for your buck? Even natural light gardens can use some of the following extra touches that increase the productivity of your setup.

Reflective Screens

Line the perimeter of your garden with simple reflective screens. Doing so will increase the intensity of the light by twenty to fifty percent. The screens bounce stray light back towards the plants, thus increasing the amount of light available to them. Window gardens in which the light comes from one direction can benefit the most from reflective screens. Screens should encase electric gardens as much as possible without cutting off any air circulation.

Screens can be made from just about anything, as long as it's reflective and durable. Cardboard, Styrofoam boards, and plywood sheets are my favorites. They

A water cooled light fixture.

A light fixture cooled by forced air.

can be covered with aluminum foil, or Mylar, or painted flat white. Use existing walls if you can as they are easily wallpapered or painted. If you don't want to paint directly onto the wall, tack up some cardboard sheets and paint on those. I liked to use a corner where the two existing walls make up the back and one side, then construct removable panels for the other wall and front. Most apartment walls are painted flat white or semi gloss anyway, so they're likely already usable. Flat white is the best common paint to use it reflects more light, but greenhouse white reflects the most so it's great to use if you can find it. Plastic drop cloths make excellent curtains for the front access to most small gardens. They're easy to work with and are very durable. In a closet you can use three walls to make up the back and two sides, then use the drop cloth to construct a curtain for the front. Line the backside of the drop cloth with black plastic to eliminate any light passing through the curtain, making the white side more reflective.

Lots of people forget about the floor being a reflective surface. Most electric lamps are mounted above the plants, focusing the light downward, so by making

Timers regulate lights, ventilation and circulation fans, and any other piece of equipment that needs regular turning on and off. They can be as simple as a twenty four hour dial or a more complicated multiday digital model.

the floor reflective you have reclaimed precious light that would have gotten away. Small plants and lower growth benefit the most from floor reflection.

Light Movers

Light movers do exactly what their name implies: they physically move a lamp, or combination of lamps around in a precise and mechanical manner. By doing so, one lamp may do the work of two or more. A grower may also create a balanced spectrum by mixing different lamps. Light movers come in several models: rails, whirligigs, and arms.

Rails move one or two lamps along a track, effectively doubling the amount of garden space. The best place for a light rail is a skinny garden that is wider than it is deep.

Whirligigs move one or more lamps in a circle around a fixed point. This is one of the best ways to mix spectrums. A unit with a 1,000-watt HPS and a 1,000-watt MH allows any ten-foot circle of bedroom space to yield a pound of bud or more every harvest.

Arms move a single lamp in an arc or circle, depending on the model. Most come with only a single lamp fixture, but some do use duel fixture models that could blend spectrums.

Timers

Timers are essential in electrical gardens, as they turn lamps, fans, and CO2 tanks on and off in a safe and dependable manner. This allows the grower to concentrate on more important matters.

Now, you may think that a timer is an unnecessary waste of forty dollars when you could simply turn the lights on and off by hand. Don't kid yourself. A timer is something every grower should invest in, because the plants need a very strict light schedule and failure to provide them with one will result in very confused plants that may not flower. Some lamps like the high-powered HIDs also need timers to turn them off safely; pulling the plug yourself is tough on the equipment and may even give you a shock.

Different timers are rated for different electrical needs. You don't want to run a 1,000-watt lamp on a wimpy power source because it could cause a dangerous fire.

Extensions Cords and Power Strips

Most gardens need wall sockets and you hardly ever find enough to run everything

Lesson 1.7: *Light*

in an electrical garden. So just like timers, extension cords and power strips have become important fixtures in indoor gardens.

Always invest in cords that are rated at higher wattages than the equipment used. This way you shouldn't develop a problem. The rating for how much electricity a cord can handle is listed either on the cord itself or on the packaging it comes with.

Coolant Fans

Electrical light and ballasts produce heat, which negatively affects the plants if allowed to build up too much. To avoid this happening when using lots of lights, every garden needs good ventilation and the air must be kept moving. Hot gardens increase the plants' demand for water, and if the room becomes too humid, insect and fungus/mold problems begin to mushroom.

The best cure for this is a simple rotation fan. Mount or position it so that it blows a strong current over the plants, but not directly on them. If the fan blows directly on the plants it will dry them out and create a condition known as windburn. The idea is to make the branches move with strong indirect currents of air.

Small coolant fans mounted to the light fixtures are very useful. An eight-inch fan blowing a carpet of cool air directly onto the bulb or between the bulb and the plant tops will allow the plants to grow much closer to the light. I used to be able to place my hand on top of my lamp fixture, and it only felt warm; my plants could grow within a foot of the bulb. I also suggest using a small fan to cool ballasts. By keeping the equipment cool the overall temperature of the garden is lowered, and the life of the equipment is extended. Middle management suck-up types call this a "win-win situation."

Chapter Summary

The type of light cycle your plants are exposed to will determine which type of growth they produce.

Long light cycles will produce vegetative growth, while short cycles will produce floral growth.

The minimum amount of electric light needed is twenty watts per square foot of growth.

There are several types of electric lamps available, but consider using fluorescents for sprouting and HIDs for later growth. LEDs can offer a cost-effective long-term lighting investment.

Use reflective screens to get the most out of your light sources.

Terms to Learn
- Floral growth
- Vegetative growth
- Fluorescents
- Incandescent
- Ballast

Hydroponics

You have probably heard that hydro-grown marijuana is more potent than soil-grown. This is a myth. A good soil system can produce the same quality growth as a hydroponic system.

Water culture basically means growing plants in a non-organic, or non-soil, environment. All nutrients are delivered directly to the plants by water in a systematic and often mechanical manner. The root ball of the plant is supported by a non-soil medium like rock wool, flora foam, lava rocks, perlite, or expanded clay pellets. Sometimes the root may be suspended in a flow of water by mechanical means, such as collars or baskets. Hydroponic plants may be grown in individual, self-contained units similar to soil pots, or housed several at a time in large troughs, trays, or PVC pipe setups.

Passive Systems

Simple Hand Feed System

Each time you deliver nutrients to your plants in a water-soluble fertilizer, you are using hydroponics; just because there is dirt in the pot it doesn't mean it's organic. In fact, most organic growers give their plants booster doses of fertilizer, usually prior to a change in the plant's life cycle.

Wick System

In wick systems, a water/nutrient basin is situated below the plant containers. The bottoms of the plant containers are elevated a couple of inches above the waterline. The water, nutrients and oxygen travel up through wicks to the plants by capillary action. Wick systems are very easy to use and worth learning about, as they can be used in both hydroponics and soil mediums. If you don't go with an active system, use a wick system.

Nylon cords make the best wicks because they don't rot in the way that cotton or other natural fibers do. I like to use half-inch or three-eighths-inch cord, and it is necessary to use many wicks: at least two per gallon of medium. If your garden is particularly hot, try using three or four wicks per gallon of medium. Remember: you can't "over wick" but you can "under wick"!

Nutrient Application Rate

For Vegetative Stage:

week	ml per litre	ml per gallon
1	2.5ml	10ml
2	4ml	15ml
3	5ml	20ml
4	7ml	25ml

For Vegetative Stage:

week	ml per litre	ml per gallon
1	7.5ml	30ml
2	7.5ml	30ml
3	7.5ml	30ml
4	7.5ml	30ml
5	7.5ml	30ml
6	7.5ml	30ml
7	flush (feed plants only water)	
8	flush (feed plants only water)	

Installing a Wick System

First cut, punch, or melt any holes that your plant container may need, then cut the wicks to around four or six feet long. They should be long enough that they coil on the bottom of the basin while having enough length to vein their way through the medium. Melt the tips so that they won't fray while you're working with them. The end that sits in the water basin should always be melted or tied in a knot. Feed the cords through the base of the secondary containers, and tie a knot in the cord to prevent it from slipping back through the hole. After that, unravel the cords so they can form a fine network of veins throughout the medium.

Slowly fill the bucket with its medium, and while you're doing so, carefully distribute the wicks to ensure that the medium will receive equal amounts of water. Don't allow the wicks to stick up through the medium; keep them about an inch or two below the surface. Now all you have to do is keep the lower reservoir filled with water.

If you're using several buckets you might find it easier to connect all your reservoir containers to one centralized control container. Use three-eighths gauge flexible hoses, and plumber's epoxy to make the seals watertight. Add the water to the control bucket and it will travel through the tubes and fill the other reservoir containers. A mature plant can drink up to a gallon of water each day. Several of them can drain a control bucket several times in a twenty-four hour period. To lengthen the times between watering (for instance, if you're going on vacation) attach a water reservoir automated with a simple toilet float valve.

The float valve is mounted in the central control bucket and connects to the water reserve with three-eights flexible plastic tubing. When the water level falls in the control bucket, the valve is tripped and refills the water. Depending on how big your reservoir is, and how much of a water demand you have, you could go away for a few days or even a week without any problems.

A variation on the wick system can be produced in the following manner. First prepare the containers as normal, then instead of the tubing and individual reservoir containers, place the medium buckets over a large community basin and dangle the wicks into it. Large basins such as kiddy pools work really well. Support the plant containers with bricks or wooden pallets. The plants feed out of one large pool and all you have to do is keep it full. The system can be automated in the same manner as the reservoir bucket above.

Lesson 1.8: *Hydroponics*

Step-by-step: How to Build A Wick System

1. Wick cordage.

2. Inter-fitting containers.

3. Cordage through container.

4. Secure cordage.

5 Cordage drapes into water

6. Put the plant inside.

7. Wick will feed roots.

8. Water soluble fertilizer.

9. Always mix well.

DIY Hydroponics

Simple hydro set up.

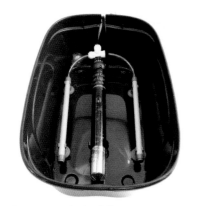

Water and air feed lines.

Lid with eight plant spaces.

Active Systems

Aeration Systems

Similar to the wick system, in an aeration system the root ball is housed in an individual container filled with a non-organic medium. This time, however, the container is not suspended above the water, but partially submerged in it. Roots grow out of the containers and directly into the surrounding water. This gives the plants the illusion of growing in a really big container, so they will no longer require additional transplanting.

Wicks are no longer necessary to supply oxygen; this is done by a simple aquarium air pump. Because the roots grow out of the containers and into the surrounding water reservoir, the plants' containers don't need to be very large. The best to use are cheap plastic one-gallon nursery containers but just about anything similar will work. I once used one-gallon water jugs with the tops cut off. They cost about a dollar each at the grocery store, and the handle made it much easier to move them around.

In my opinion, an aeration system is the best choice for those taking their first steps into the world of hydroponics. They are pretty much idiot-proof, require little upfront spending, and are very effective.

Nutrient Film or Nutrient Flow Technique (NFT)

Most NFTs consist of pipes that have individual holes for the plants to sit in. Water is constantly flowing through the bottom of the pipes, while the root ball sits above the flow of water with only the root tips dangling down into the shallow flow below. Because the water is constantly kept moving, there is no need for an air pump or timer.

Ebb and Flow System

In this kind of system, a pump and timer are used to periodically flood a tray in which the plants are situated. Several plants can be lined in rows, usually in blocks of rock wool. Water drains out of the tray by the force of gravity. It is fed back to a reservoir where the pump can re-circulate it to the tray at the next designated time.

Aeroponics

Aeroponic systems differ from hydroponic systems in that the roots dangle midair in a pipe or similar chamber, supported by collars or baskets, and a pump pushes water to sprayers that constantly mist the roots. As in the Ebb and Flow technique, the water flows to a reservoir where it can be recycled.

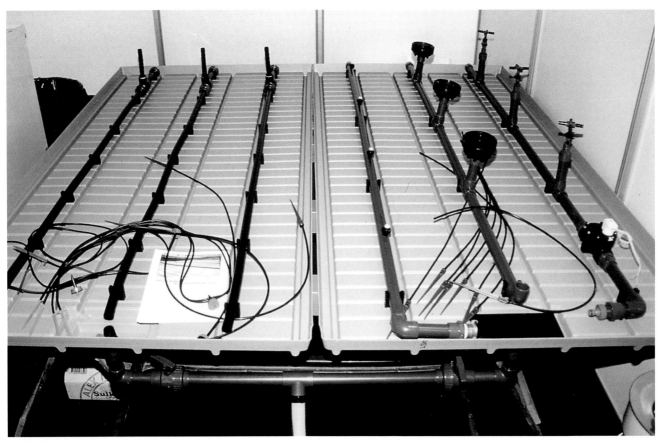

Drip irrigation systems can maintain a lot of plants, but the emitters will need to be regularly maintained and adjusted.

Drip Systems

A pump sends the water solution through a system of hoses to drip emitters situated at the base of each plant. The water trickles through the medium and into a reservoir where it can be pumped again later. Some experience is required to adjust the drippings correctly, and as the plants grow, the dripping rate will need further adjustment.

Build One Yourself

All of these systems work very well when employed properly, but out of all of them the easiest to setup is the aeration garden. It was the simplest hydroponics system I ever used, and was very uncomplicated to construct and operate.

This grower used a BC Northern Lights hydroponic system to produce an incredible harvest.

Tip!

The experts at BC Northern Lights suggest using baking soda for pH Up and lemon juice for pH Down if you cannot get the real stuff from an aquarium shop or a pool supply store.

In addition, white plastic sheeting can act as a basin cover, so it's handy to have. Air pumps are the lungs of the garden. They are available at any pet shop in the aquarium department and are cheap at about twenty dollars for the basic model. Their function is to prevent the water from becoming stagnant or void of oxygen. If using many basins, multiple pumps and hose dividers are required to oxygenate all the plants. With one large basin one pump can do the job, but I suggest using at least two, as the plants receive more oxygen, and if a pump fails or is dislodged, the other acts as a backup. Remember: you can't over oxygenate the water. Always position the pumps above the water level. This will reduce the strain

*Lesson 1.8: **Hydroponics***

on the pumps, greatly increasing their output and life span.

Air stones and diffusers simply break up the flow of air coming out of the hose. They cost a dollar for the small ones and ten dollars for the larger, foot-long models. Some air stones come in flexible tube models that can snake between containers. The tiny bubbles supply more air to the water, and help reduce the noise. They are not a luxury, but instead are standard components. If using one stone per basin, position it in the center. If two, place them evenly in the basin to distribute the flow of oxygen equally.

Hosing is very cheap; no more than ten cents per foot. Most pet stores carry bundles of ten, twenty, or fifty feet. DIY stores carry bulk amounts. Be sure to only use enough hosing as required, because slack, or uneven lengths of hosing, will lead to lower air pressure. Run and secure hosing along walls or chamber framework.

Basins hold the water reservoir. The secondary containers sit in the basin with the lower inch or two submerged in the water. The roots grow through the medium and out into the reservoir. There are advantages to using larger community basins instead of many smaller individual water trays. All the plants' water needs can be taken care of at the same time, and there isn't an octopus of tangled air hoses. Anything from a plastic drawer to a kiddy pool can make a good basin as long as it's black, plastic, waterproof, and at least twice as deep as the waterline. Basins should always be black, as this discourages algae growth. If you can't find black, use trash bags or sheeting to line the basins. Basins get knocked around and scratched a lot; plastic absorbs this stress.

A cheap custom basin can be made out of a framework of wood and many layers of plastic sheeting. It's best to use as many layers as possible, but be sure to use no less than ten. If you think you have enough layers, add four more. Replace damaged sheets with every crop. After one crop I discovered that half of the plastic sheets I used had been punctured. I tried this type of jury-rigged basin to see how well it worked, and I don't recommend it. It's just not worth the risk of a spill or flood. If you live in an upstairs apartment you never want to get a visit from a landlord or maintenance guy investigating a leak complaint.

Secondary containers will create support for the plants. The best are the standard one-gallon black plastic nursery containers. I like these because they are plentiful, cheap, and easy to work with. While passing a nursery store one day I saw a worker throwing away hundreds of used containers. I asked if they were for sale and he told me I could help myself, so I snagged two hundred. I gave

Essential Components for Building Your System

- One or two aquarium pumps
- Enough hosing and air stones to meet your needs
- One or more water basins
- Enough secondary containers to occupy the basins)
- Enough non-organic medium to fill the secondary containers
- Water-soluble fertilizers
- A pH tester
- pH adjusters if needed)
- A mixing pail or plastic milk jug

Tip!

When using a hydroponic system it's best to change your water every two weeks to stop bacteria growth and ensure your plants are receiving fresh water.

most away to other growers, but kept fifty for myself. If you have to make your own secondary containers use them as the example. Containers need to have at least four three-eighths-inch holes cut around the bottom sides. They should be spaced evenly apart. Sand edges smooth to prevent root snagging. A standard substitute would be one-gallon milk or water jugs with the tops cut off.

For any hydroponic system, the medium, of course, needs to be inorganic, and also should be heavy enough to supply a good foundation for the plants. I find that lava rocks are the cheapest and most effective medium. A fifty-pound bag costs about five dollars. Other effective mediums are white driveway stones or pea gravel. Professional garden stores carry expanded clay tablets that work really well, but they are expensive: around twenty dollars per cubic foot. Finer mediums or substrates are required to begin plants, and are easily transferred into the secondary containers from starter gardens. The most common are vermiculite, perlite, and rock wool.

This simple aeroponic system will produce awesome results.

Lesson 1.8: *Hydroponics*

Drip systems provide direct nutrient delivery to each individual plant.

Fertilizers supply the elemental compounds required for life and growth. There are hundreds of brands and formulas on the market. The ones to use are water-soluble, supply all nutrients, major and minor, and also have the proper balance of chemical ratios. See the chapter on nutrients to get an idea of nutrient needs and the ratios required. To prevent overdosing, try using half strength formulas, and change out the water every two to three weeks.

Clean basins with every crop to remove excessive salt deposits. Salt deposits appear as white chalky lines marking the water level. These salts affect the pH

Warning!

Do not mix pH Up and pH Down solutions directly together and do not put your electric pH tester more than an inch or so below the surface of the liquid – the testers are not waterproof.

PPM for your Grow

- Seedlings around 50-150 PPM
- Unrooted clones around 100-350 PPM
- Small plants around 400-800 PPM
- Large plants around 900-1800 PPM
- Last week of flowering use plain water

This coliseum grow system resembles the hanging gardens of Babylon.

Lesson 1.8: *Hydroponics*

and nutrient levels of the water. Always try to do a very thorough job, but don't be discouraged if the stuff never completely comes off, as this is common.

Basin covers are a great idea for this type of system. If the garden loses a lot of water, then every drop becomes valuable; in hot grow rooms, simple evaporation shortens times between watering dramatically. To combat this, use white plastic sheets or bucket lids to cover the medium around the base of each plant. Design these covers so they can be removed easily. Larger sheets can span over water basins and tables. Cut holes to allow for the secondary containers. Secure the back and sides to the basin or table. Leave the front unattached so you can lift it to add water or perform maintenance. Conversely, you could secure all the way around and cut a hole to pour the water in. If you do this I suggest using a funnel to prevent spilling the water when you add it.

Chapter Summary

Any soil-free system in which nutrients are delivered to plants in a systematic manner is a hydroponic system.

Passive hydro systems include Simple Hand Feed systems and Wick systems.

Active hydro systems include Aeration systems, NFTs, and Ebb and Flow systems.

Aeroponics differs from hydroponics as the plants' roots hang in air rather than water.

Terms to Learn

- Rock wool
- Perlite
- Wick system
- Aeration
- Nutrient Flow Technique
- Ebb and Flow

Lesson 1.9

Soils, Substrates, and Media

For most beginners, it feels natural to start with soil because it is cheap, readily available, and can be more forgiving than a hydroponic system. Growers are divided on the subject of which of the two systems grows the best buds. For the most part, it's generally agreed that hydroponic systems produce faster-growing plants, and allow for a more precise control over the garden's nutrient needs, while plants grown in organic-based systems can have a more pleasant tasting smoke. Also, soil systems provide a natural buffering system against some fertilizer and pH mistakes. In truth, there is no superior way to grow marijuana. It comes down to the preference of the grower, just as some artists prefer to work in oils and some in marble. Use the method that makes the most sense to you and your situation.

Soil and Organic

It may be a hard concept to understand, but not all dirt is considered organic. Many products on the market are really just mixtures of sand, bark, and a few substrates. Real organic farming means that the soil has been fortified with natural matter rich in nutrients, and that microorganisms have processed this into a form that the plants can absorb and utilize. This conversion process is a lot like the bacteria in our digestive tract that helps us digest food. It can take weeks or even months for the microorganisms to convert the matter. When properly prepared, plants thrive in organic mixes, and all the grower has to do is add pH-adjusted, nutrient-free water.

The main problem with organics is that the supply of nutrients is limited and will eventually be used up.

Another problem is the disposal of soil after each crop. Never reuse soil or additives from previous crops, as they can carry strong nutrient salt buildups, or

Transplanting

Three layers of medium: Perlite, potting soil, and peat moss on top.

Place the rootball into the new medium so that its original surface level is maintained.

Always water a new transplant generously to prevent shock and to firm up the soil.

Start several seeds to ensure at least one viable sprout per starter cup.

diseases that could wreak havoc with the new crop. If you live in an apartment or a close-knit community then your neighbors may wonder why you need a ton of potting soil every few weeks. If this isn't a problem for you, then a soil-based system will make an excellent choice.

The Right Soils

Lets start with the basics: what kind of dirt is right for you? The perfect soil mix is loose and drains water quickly, yet retains just the right amount of moisture to suit the plants' needs. It must also have a mid-range pH of about 6.8. The

Lesson 1.9: *Soils, Substrates, and Media*

These rooted clones are ready to be transplanted into larger containers.

Fix!

When the supply of nutrients in your organic medium is used up, there are two things you can do: You can either transfer the plants to larger containers with more enriched soil, or fertilize them with a water-soluble fertilizer.

best soil to start with is a professional potting soil mix of the sort you can buy at nurseries and most grocery stores. Rich professional potting soil has a fine grade to it, like coffee grinds, with very few chunks of bark or rocks. These soils are sometimes referred to as "soilless" because they really don't have actual dirt in them. Typical mixtures are made from peat, sand, lime, perlite, vermiculite, and some low-level slow-release nutrients. These soils come in bags of various sizes, ranging from small eight-quart to larger twenty-five, forty, or even fifty pound ones. Eight-quart bags cost around four to five dollars, and will fill two gallon-size nursery containers.

Tip!

Always lay a plastic tarp down if you are amending your soil or growing medium indoors. Dirt is, well, dirty, and it can make a real mess of your grow area if you're not careful! Cleanliness is key. Some growers go so far as to do all their medium mixing in the bathtub!

Additives

Even "ready to use" name brand potting soils can use a few little extras to give the plants some extra help, so be ready to invest in several different bags of ingredients. Thankfully they're cheap; you'll only spend twenty or thirty dollars for a small operation.

Perlite

Perlite consists of small pieces of pumice, a volcanic rock, and is almost always bright white. It is inert and loosens soil really well. I recommend it in all soil mixes to ensure proper water drainage, and it can also be used on its own to sprout seeds or root clones. Some hydroponic systems use a hundred percent perlite as a growth medium, but as it is so light, unsupported plants may fall over. In addition, perlite can be used as a draining medium in the bottoms of containers as long as the drain holes aren't too large.

Vermiculite

Vermiculite is basically mica that has been puffed in an oven, kind of like popcorn. It both loosens the soil and improves water retention. It holds both air and water like a sponge and, like perlite, can be used by itself to sprout seedlings and root clones.

Topsoil

Topsoil is the soil you find under the grass in your front yard. It's just a simple mix of wood by-products, sand, and decayed matter such as lawn clippings and bark. Topsoil by itself is a poor growth medium for weed, because it clumps up into pieces and can harden like a rock when it gets too dry. Topsoil should only be used as a basic fill in your medium, and should always be loosened up with added mediums.

Compost

Hand-made compost is a rich mix of fully decayed organic matter. It can contain anything and everything, from coffee grinds to last year's crop. Compost should be well matured and free of non-decomposed material. Depending on how rich in nutrients it is, you may never have to fertilize. Commercial compost is more or less just ground up vegetative matter, leaving it quite low in nutrients and in need of regular fertilization.

Soil Additives

Perlite

Vermiculite

Peat Moss

Topsoil

Worm Castings

Blood Meal

Rockwool

Sand

Bone Meal

Organic mix one

- 4 parts soil
- 3 parts perlite
- 2 parts peat
- 1 part manure
- 1 part wood ash

Organic mix two

- 3 parts soil
- 1 part perlite
- 1 part vermiculite
- 1 part worm castings
- 1 part manure

Peat Moss or Sphagnum

Peat and sphagnum are mosses made of dried plant matter that have been sterilized with steam to kill any little nasties. They can hold about a third their weight in water, and may have a low pH of 3.5 to 4.5 and so can help adjust an alkaline water source or soil. Alkaline soils and waters are common in the midwestern states, so keep this in mind if you are trying to adjust the pH of your water.

Sand

Sand loosens soil and allows for excellent drainage. It's free of nutrients and has a neutral pH. Some hydroponics growers use sand-only mediums in their systems, as the only drawbacks are its heavy weight and tendency to be very messy to work with. Never use beach sand because it may be polluted with salts or other toxins. Look in home improvement stores for the kind used for mixing concrete and filling children's sandboxes.

Rock wool

Rock wool looks and feels like fiberglass, but it is actually made from granite, limestone, or coke that has been heated and spun like thread. Soil gardeners can use rock wool to start plants and then transfer them to soil filled containers later. Always wet rock wool before handling it because the dust fibers can do serious damage to lungs. Some hydroponic gardeners may use rock wool as the only medium in their system.

Organic Teas

Organic teas are made of nutrients dissolved into water and are fed directly to the plants. They provide mild fertilizer feeding and can help maintain the tastiness of the smoke. Teas are simple to use and are readily found at most nurseries, or easily made at home. Organic teas are usually made from seaweed, bat guano, pecans, or worm castings.

Raw Manure

Manure is simply animal poop. The best poops for growing plants come from herbivores like cows, horses, chickens and so forth. Don't use carnivore poop, or your own for that matter, even if you only eat carrots and drink wheat grass. Manure provides a good low-grade nutrient mixture that can produce fantastic results. You don't want to use too much, though, as this will overload the plants

Lesson 1.9: *Soils, Substrates, and Media*

Step-by-step: Herbal Organic Tea Fertilizer

1. Comfrey, alfalfa and nettles.

2. Add in boiling water.

3. Steep for ten minutes.

4. Wait until lukewarm.

5. Add to spray bottle.

6. Spray leaves or add to soil.

with nutrients and burn them. In a soil mixture, one or two parts manure is a safe amount to use.

Worm Castings

Worms munch their way through the ground eating whatever organic matter comes their way and then poop out little pellets called worm castings. Worm castings, then, are a type of manure, but growers sometimes put them in their own category because they're such a good nutrient source. Worm castings alone can be used as the growth medium without burning the plants, but this may lead to water drainage problems.

Sprouts in shallow starter trays need to be transplanted as soon as they emerge.

Lesson 1.9: *Soils, Substrates, and Media*

Step-by-step: Watering with Fertilizer

1. Measure out fertilizer.

2. Add water slowly.

3. Mix carefully.

4. Add to soil.

Tip!

Be careful not to get liquid on the leaves of your plants when you water them. The water itself can cause burn damage from the lights, and if you enrich your water with a fertilizer, the nitrogen can cause leaf burns if not cleaned off right away.

Mixing Soils

When mixing soils be sure to wet them as, like rock wool, the dust given off can irritate ones lungs. Use a simple painter's mask to protect yourself when mixing large quantities.

Mixing can be very messy, so use a basin to work in. A bathtub lined with plastic or a small plastic kiddy pool is the best option when working with a large amount of soil. A large five-gallon bucket is sufficient for preparing smaller amounts. It may seem like hard work to mix and measure your mediums, but look at it this way: you're preparing a home for your plants. The better the mix, the better the eventual results. Be sure to remove any stones, large pieces of bark, twigs or

This massive root is loving life in its healthy grow medium with Perlite additives.

other litter, as well as breaking up any large lumps and clumps.

On page 92 there are two good basic organic mixes that work very well. Try them before you begin to experiment with your whole grow. Remember that the plants may quickly use up the nutrients, so you may have to fertilize them a little. For reference, a "part" is based on whatever you are using to scoop the ingredients with. It could be your hand, a drink cup, or anything else.

Hydroponic Mixes

For a hydroponic mix, just about anything inorganic will work well. I liked to use black lava rocks because they were heavy enough to provide support for the plants, and didn't mess with the nutrient or pH levels. Styrofoam peanuts also work well, as does pea gravel. Grow shops often sell overpriced grow mediums that you can live without if you simply shop around. The only medium I ever bought from a grow shop was rock wool, because it works so well with clones. However, it also draws unwanted attention to you and, for this reason, should be avoided when possible. Try using a fifty-fifty mixture of perlite and vermiculite as a replacement.

Inorganic Mixes

Inorganic soil mixes require a water-based fertilizer to supply all nutrients. These may be the best way for you to start on that first experimental crop. Later, when you have more confidence, you can move on to more complicated organic mixes. This method is really a form of hydroponic farming, as all the nutrients are supplied via the water and the soil medium is just there to provide support for the plants.

Chapter Summary

While hydroponic systems can boost plant growth, soil systems are more forgiving to error.

All soil systems can benefit from added mediums such as perlite, compost, or sand.

Producing an organic soil mix can give great results and ensure a steady flow of nutrients to your plants.

Terms to Learn
- Manure
- Worm castings
- Compost
- Peat moss
- Sphagnum

Bending and Pruning

The first step to controlling plant height should be taken just after the plants pass through the delicate seedling stage. By this time, the plants should be almost a foot tall, and the lower branches should be developing nicely. Now you have to make an important decision: should you first remove the lower branches and force the plant to grow only one large top bud, or should you clip the top shoot and allow the lower branches to grow up, making many smaller buds?

How big you want to make the plant depends on three things: how many you feel comfortable growing, the size of the space you have to growing in, and how long you are willing to wait. For instance, you can grow 16 plants in a four-foot square area: one for each square foot. On the other hand, you could grow four plants in the same area by spacing them one for every two square feet.

If you choose to grow many small plants, I suggest using the single top bud method. By removing the lower growth, the plant puts all its energy into the main bud, which therefore grows quite large. If you're only growing a few plants, I suggest training them as bushy plants. It may seem insane to cut the heads off your babies, but it allows the lower branches to grow up, and the plants can then be staked out to fill the garden space. The drawback to growing fewer, larger plants is that it will take longer to mature them.

In the past half-century, marijuana breeders have crossbred different strains from around the world. The resulting hybrids have developed many specific patterns of behavior. This, coupled with environmental variations, means that some plants in a garden may grow faster than the others. If you don't keep an eye on things, a few plants may dominate your garden and choke the rest out.

Single Cola Tech

Single-stalk plants have a tendency to fall over from the weight of their buds, so

Proper Staking Technique

Be sure to stake your plants so that they can support the weight of their own buds. Bamboo poles make good stakes.

you may have to create support for them. The easiest way to do this is to stick a bamboo stake or similar into the medium, right next to the plant, and tie the stalk to it. Plants with larger buds may need two or more stakes.

Bushes or Maxi-cropping

Making bushes is sometimes called maxi-cropping. It's a simple procedure: just remove the top shoot, and allow the lower branches to grow up. The earliest point at which to remove the top growth is about three weeks into growing. By this time, the plants should be about a foot tall and have several sets of branch internodes.

Training

Training gives the grower control over the plants' height and shape. Under electric light it's important to keep all the plants at an even height. This is where the term

This well-trained plant is anchored to its own container, making it easy to move and care for.

Methods of Training and Bending Your Plants

Tie cords to solid objects.

Fix securely.

Gently bend plant.

Focal point of the fixture.

Plant bent in all directions.

Bent plant catches more light.

Very careful bending.

Bending and controlling Sativa.

Trained plants produce more bud.

Lesson 1.10: *Bending and Pruning*

"sea of green" (SOG) comes from, because the even carpet of level buds tops appears like a calm green ocean.

By fanning out bushy plants you expose more of the lower growth to your light source. When encouraged, these plants produce more bud at harvest than plants with crowded, light-starved undergrowth.

To spread large main branches you can use one of three basic methods. The first is similar to the method used for bending small stems. Use a combination of strong cord or twine and tape. Loop the tape around the selected branch and then use string or cord to tie it off. Anchor the other end of the cord to either a heavy object or to the container itself. Using bricks or other heavy objects to anchor the cord allows you to spread branches out over a larger area than tying them to the

Bending Your Plant

Knot the string around the base of your plant and twine it up the stalk and about ¾ of the way along one of the larger branches. Then attach the string to a weight in order to bend the plant in the direction you need it to go. Be gentle and don't break any branches. It should take about a week to get her stabilized.

Dinafem Seeds have a beautiful grow room.

Buds supported by netting.

Healthy bud.

container, but using the plant container as the anchor makes it easier for you to move or rotate the plant.

The second spreading technique requires building a skeleton framework, or "cage," and training the plant to grow along it. Tomatoes are often grown in metal cages that provide plant support and ease of pruning. I made similar cages with bamboo and twine. Mount four bamboo stakes evenly around the container by taping them to the outside. Avoid sticking wooden stakes into the medium, as they will eventually rot. Tie several cords to the stakes in the manner of boxing ring ropes. The plant can be tied to the cage, thus controlling its shape and supporting its heavy budding branches. To widen the cage for larger plants, attach more stakes horizontally to the frame and train the plant on it.

Beautiful crop of Valley Queen by No Mercy Supply.

Fix!

Sometimes a few plants will dominate the garden and choke the rest of the plants out. To correct this, the first thing to do is to place the smaller plants under the center of the lights. This way, they are exposed to stronger light and have a chance to catch up with the taller ones. You could also try elevating the smaller plants on books, boxes, bricks, or other planting containers. A novel idea is to line up the plants by height and tilt the light source to illuminate them equally. This method works well with fluorescent tubes that naturally conform to odd spaces.

The third method simply involves hanging a net or support line of nylon strings across the entire garden. The plants gain support by growing up through the netting. The disadvantage is that the plants can't be moved around or rotated once they grow up through the net, but if that's not a problem for you it can be a fantastic system, as it's much easier to erect one net then several individual cages.

Twin Towers

In this situation, you simply grow two buds on the top of the plant instead of one. To do this, remove the plant's top and when the next two new shoots start growing, remove the remaining lower branch growth. If there are more than two top shoots growing, remove the extra ones.

This plant by No Mercy Supply was maxi cropped and split under the weight at harvest. The bud was great!

Lesson 1.10: *Bending and Pruning*

Bending results in a shorter plant with a row of excellent bud growth.

Basic Bending for Maximum Buds

During pre-flowering and early flowering I strongly suggest bending the plants to encourage larger buds. The process is very simple; all you will need are some twisty-ties. By bending the stems, you force them to grow thicker and stronger capable of supporting larger bud heads. If you choose to use something other than twisty-ties, be careful not to use a thin surface like sewing thread or fishing line, as such a line will saw into the stem and damage the plant. Stems and branches can be trained to form several basic shapes like the classic "L," or "S," and sometimes even a complete circle.

Chapter Summary

Bending or pruning your plants will control their height and force them to grow either one large top bud or many smaller ones, depending on your preference.

A single-cola tech can be created by removing the lower growth to force a huge top bud. This is good for smaller plants.

When maxi-cropping, remove the top bud to force bushier plants laden with many smaller buds.

Training plants makes best use of the light source and space. Sea of Green and Screen of Green are both popular training methods.

Terms to Learn
- Hybrid
- Cola
- Maxi-cropping
- Sea of Green (SoG)
- Screen of Green (ScroG)

Strains

You may not know exactly what you are growing but this crash course will help. As we discussed earlier in the book, marijuana is divided into two main species. Sativa plants are traditionally larger with longer growth cycles, renowned for their soaring "spiritual" head high. Indica plants are generally more compact, with shorter growing cycles, and they pack a premium power high. When smoking the two, one may find it difficult to pick a personal preference, but when growing indoors the mass majority of growers find that indicas are the clear-cut choice. Indica/sativa hybrids abound, and may display any combination of traits.

Which is Which?

I won't pretend to know everything about every strain of marijuana on the planet, but I will say that I knew what I liked when I smoked it, and that's the place to start. Save seeds from the stuff you enjoy. When you have a nice seed collection, start growing. You may eventually find a special lady that you want to clone and grow crop after crop with. The following is a general description of traditional strains from different countries and continents. Marijuana is one of the most diverse plants in the world, and there are hybrids of every variety. Don't worry too much about specifics; the only real way to find out what kind of plant you're going to get is to grow it. If you're happy with the results you get, and you're not looking to move into serious breeding, then forget about trying to identify its origins and kick back, relax, and enjoy what you've got.

Sativa Strains

Sativa plants yield from a third of a pound to five pounds of sinsemilla (non-seeded buds) per plant outside in full sunlight. Sativas are generally larger plants with light green leaves and long narrow blades. As mentioned before, these plants traditionally have a longer maturation cycle than other types of Cannabis, such as Indica or Ruderalis. Sativas do fairly well in tropical climates, where they take advantage of the longer growing seasons. Sativas ripen in mid-October through December. In Central America, near the equator, some plants have been known to live for several

Top of Their Class: Sativa Strains

World of Seeds: Wild Thailand.

World of Seeds: Kilimanjaro.

Sensi Seeds: Mexican Sativa.

Landrace Swazi from South Africa.

Delta 9 Labs: Mekong Haze.

Landrace Malawi growing wild.

Alpine Seeds: Nepalese.

Landrace Durban Poison, South Africa.

Green House Seed Co.: Hawaiian Snow.

years switching back and forth between vegetative and floral stages. Sativa is usually imported from countries south of the United States, although they grow all over the world. The most common varieties imported into the States are Mexican, Colombian, and Jamaican.

Mexican

Mexican grows faster and maturates quicker than most Colombian and Jamaican. It's the staple for most U.S. smokers, and can be found from California to the Deep South in great abundance. Mexican is classified as a mild grade, which a lot of smokers like because it gives them just the right buzz without completely debilitating them. It forms a conical or "Christmas tree" shape which is beautiful to look at and is ideal for outdoor growers. The growth can be dense and full under strong light, and the plants can form fat colas if grown properly. The flowers produced by Mexican Sativas are almost always white.

Colombian

Colombian grows and matures slower than most Mexican and Jamaican. The plants can form a distinct diamond shape, with white flowers. This variety is a real pain to grow under electric lights, because after flowering begins the plants can easily double or triple their height. When they grow too large, too quickly, they can run out of space in a small grow room. However, if your environment permits, and you have the patience, Colombian may be the best smoke you can grow. It has a really powerful high that is both relaxing and soulful.

Jamaican

The original "ganja," Jamaican's growth, potency, and maturation fall somewhere between Mexican and Colombian. Typical Jamaican plants form conical shapes like Mexicans, but the branches are better defined, with thinner buds and colas. Flowers are also traditionally white, but the occasional red will show up.

African

The only example of marijuana from Africa that I've ever seen was Nigerian. The plant had a deep plain green color, and the leaves were very long, thin, and sharp. The body was thick with an oblong profile. It had many branches with extremely compact internodal spacing. Overall, the plant stood around five feet tall with well-formed colas. The flowers were mostly white with just a hint of pink. The smoke

Cannabis Sativa

Sativa plants are taller, with longer, thinner leaves and light green coloration. Even the buds are long and thin (and delicious!) Typically, a Sativa plant will have a sweet, fruity taste and the smoke is fairly mild — that is to say, it gets you 'high' but it does not get you 'stoned'. So, like the plant itself, which is tall, light and airy, the effects of smoking Sativa are lighter, and more conscious. It is a head high, not a body high.

Smoke Report

When you smoke a Sativa plant, you get more of a cerebral high. Sativa makes you want to talk to people, have fun, and sometimes be creative. The taste is often sweet and fruity, and very mild, although the effects can be quite intense. Sativa wakes you up.

This plant is looking very healthy and has a gorgeous crown of pistils beginning to appear.

tasted woody and gave an energetic almost immediate punch. A popular strain from South Africa is called Durban Poison, and is said to be a really good producer. The connoisseurs at South Africa's premier online Cannabis forum, weed.co.za, inform me that Durban Poison grows wild in the Durban region of South Africa, and it is a delicious, fast finishing Sativa. Locals call the weed in Africa "dagga" or "majut," but everyone else just calls it incredible. Africa is an enormous continent, and the cannabis is as diverse as the people and cultures.

Asian

Asian sativa should be avoided for growing because of high levels of natural hermaphrodite mutations associated with those strains. Asian pot is sometimes marketed in Thai stick form. Loose collections of buds are wrapped around a stick and secured with string. Just like Africa, Asia is a huge land with many diverse types of weed. For the most part it's all sativa, but indica actually originates from central Asia.

Indian

An exchange student I once met in Austin, TX, told me of the pot his family had been growing for generations near the city of Nagpur. He told me that the weed had a sativa-like conical profile, and averaged five to seven feet tall. The taste he described as "most sweet and tasty." The buds were loose, but very long and running.

Indica Strains

Generally shorter in height, indica plants produce up to two pounds of sinsemilla outdoors in full light. These days, "indo" is available practically everywhere, and it is almost always more expensive than the standard sativa import, but well worth the price. These cool temperature high altitude-loving plants originate from the Middle East and central Asia. Their leaves are dark green to bluish or even deep purple. Flower color can range from standard white through reds, purples, and blues. Because marijuana growers are always trying to grow the ultimate weed there are countless varieties of indica with ever more being developed.

Afghanistan

This is the original indo. Its very pungent in smell and taste, and the resin content can be quite high as it was originally bred for hash making. Afghan plants as we know them didn't exist until quite recently, when displaced refugees traveling

African Free by Eva Female Seeds is a cross between a pure South African female and an Indian male. It is a very hardy strain that has a sweet, fruity taste and a euphoric Sativa effect. Great for S.O.G. and hash extraction.

Cannabis Indica

Indica plants are short and squat, and the leaves are short and wide. The leaves are often dark green. Indica  plants are much more volatile than other types of Cannabis — that is to say, they produce a much more noticeably "skunky" odor. So, be aware when growing an Indica that air ventilation and filtration are very important. Indica smoke is thick and causes some tokers to cough if they aren't prepared for it. Indica gets you stoned and causes what is referred to as "couch lock".

Smoke Report

When you smoke an Indica plant, you get more of a "body" high. Indica makes you stoned so that you want to sit on the couch and relax. This is called "couch-lock" by experienced tokers. The taste is heavy, and the smoke is thick and hash-like. Indica smoke is intense and potent, and can help put you to sleep.

through the country collected and bred the local wide leaf wild plants with their traditional sativa. The end results were kick-ass hybrids.

Modern Strains

During the past few decades, more advances in breeding new marijuana strains have been made than in all the previous history of mankind's relationship with it. I won't even begin to try to list them all, but I will mention three that have been and will continue to be mainstays of the breeding world for the next few years.

Zensation by Ministry of Cannabis is a very potent Indica strain.

Top of Their Class: Indica Strains

World of Seeds: Pakistan Valley.

Dr. Greenthumb Seeds: Iranian Auto.

World of Seeds: Afghan Kush.

Autofem Seeds: Auto Uzbek.

Sagarmatha Seeds: Mangolian Indica.

Alpine Seeds: Landrace Afghani.

Ministry of Cannabis: Kandahar.

Dutch Passion: Ortega Indica.

Green House Seed Co.: Himalaya Gold.

Top of Their Class: Modern Hybrid Strains

World of Seeds: Mazar x White Rhino.

Vulkania Seeds: Dhaze.

Eva Female Seeds: Nexus.

Sweet Seeds: Green Poison.

Peak Seeds: Skunkberry.

Dinafem Seeds: Blue Fruit.

Ch9 Female Seeds: Ch9 Flower.

No Mercy Supply: Lucky Queen.

Alpine Seeds: Ultra Jax.

Lesson 1.11: *Strains*

Northern Lights

This is a great pure indica strain that has such infamy that most people have heard of it. It usually packs a strong stone that can render the user lethargic or immobile. The strain I grew took about four to six weeks to vegetate, and about sixty-five days to finish flowering. Forced to finish so quickly, the plants never got over twenty-four to thirty inches tall under a 430-watt HPS.

Blueberry

This is my personal favorite and I count anyone with a full bowl of this stuff as a friend. The first time I tried this particular strain I was in a Vancouver coffee shop and it stoned the shit out of me. I loved the berry taste and smell that added to the clear energetic feeling it gave. When I finally scored some pure breed seeds of it, I was impressed by the pungent smell that the plants produced. The flowering cycle took as few as forty-five to fifty days and the plants could be forced to stay under three feet. All I've been able to determine about the ancestry is that it's about seventy-five percent indica and twenty-five percent sativa.

Big Bud

Big Bud can be one of the more stubborn and difficult strains to grow as it can take more than seventy-five days to finish, but it makes up for this producing some of the biggest buds and colas possible. Problems can include low cloning success, vertical height issues, longer maturation, and even stronger lighting demand. If these weren't enough most growers have to sift through this strain to find the really outstanding performers. Typically, only one in four plants will produce the legendarily heavy buds that growers crave.

Chapter Summary

Always save seeds from marijuana that you enjoy.

Sativa plants are taller with light leaves and long narrow blades.

Indica plants are normally shorter with dark, purplish leaves. They are preferable for indoor growing due to space restrictions.

New varieties are constantly being bred.

Terms to Learn
- Northern Lights
- Blueberry
- Big Bud

Garden Examples

These are not guides for constructing gardens but examples that may give you an idea or two for your own grow space. Aspects of these gardens are interchangeable, so use your imagination and practical sense to create your own.

Window Gardens

The simplest garden is the no-frills window setup with a single spotlight added to lengthen and strengthen the light cycle. One or two more lights would be better, but reflective screens opposite the window increase light reflection in the garden for maximum results. Plastic drop cloths under the containers also help to make the most of the available light.

Closet Garden

Alcohol prohibition was overthrown because it was impossible to enforce. Despite the best efforts of police to enforce the Eighteenth Amendment, the majority of people drank to some extent and the law was corrupt as hell. Sound familiar?

Much like the marijuana version of the speakeasy, the small closet garden is easy to hide, and can be very productive, making it one of the most common setups for novice growers. The typical problems in a closet are ventilation and electrical wiring. Pay close attention to these issues and you will be well on your way to growing some amazing bud in whatever space is available to you.

Natural Light Gardens

Balconies, porches, skylight, windows, or backyards are common places to find plants basking in the sun. The most important consideration is security. If your plants are found, you'll either get arrested or ripped off. The amount of light a plant receives can also be a major concern.

Garden Design 101

Closet with reflective film.

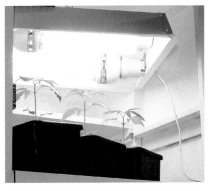

Top shelf in mini closet grow.

Closet garden with HIDs.

Window garden.

Window garden.

Balcony greenhouse.

Clandestine balcony grow.

OGA Seeds corner garden.

Stacked rotation garden.

Lesson 1.12: *Garden Examples*

Opaque curtains let light in and help keep prying eyes out.

Fix!

Every grow area is different, and every plant is different, too. If you find that one plant overshadows another in the grow room, try raising the smaller plant up by placing it on top of something and thereby closer to the light and out of the shadows. The window grow in the photo demonstrates this nicely. The smaller plants on the right have been raised about an inch to compensate for their shorter stature.

Corner Gardens

A corner in an upstairs room can be turned into a valuable piece of property. Necessary materials like white paint, cardboard boxes, plastic sheeting, hanging hooks and cord are cheap and easy to find. When you set up a corner garden, use the two walls as the back and one side and construct cheap removable screens to wall the front and final side. A little white paint on cardboard is very effective for this. Plastic sheeting can protect carpeted floors, its best to use more than one layer in case the first gets punctured.

Rotation Garden

I loved my rotation garden. It's the best system a small-time grower can use to produce a perpetual sea of green. This method doesn't cost an arm and a leg to set up and operate, as it uses a moderate amount of electricity, can be tailored to fit the grower's choice in location, and is a very low maintenance system. Mine

Warning!

Always be careful with a window or natural light garden. Your number one concern should be security: if someone can see the garden, then you have a problem. Fix it.

These plants will be moved to a different room when they are ready to flower.

required only a couple of days of real work every month: one to start a new batch of clones and another, two weeks later, to harvest and rotate the crops. Other than that, I needed to routinely prune and turn the plants to ensure even growth and health, and properly maintain the quality and nutrient level of the water.

This garden used a couple of simple aeration hydroponic buckets to house the mother plants, which were grown in one-gallon containers filled with black lava rocks. Clones were rooted in plastic drink cups using rock wool cubes and a mixture of perlite and vermiculite. The plants and clones were stacked on top of simple boxes to adjust their height as needed. The fluorescents were fixed to the underside of the

Lesson 1.12: *Garden Examples*

floral garden and the front of the garden was accessible via a rolled up curtain made from a white drop cloth and several layers of black plastic backing.

The floral garden consisted of two aeration hydroponic basins. The plants were grown in one-gallon containers filled with lava rocks just like their mothers. The 430-watt HPS lamp could be mounted less than 18 inches above the plants thanks to an aggressive heat ventilation system. Even thought the closet was small, I had just enough room to sit in front of it and smoke bowl after bowl while watching the grass grow. Towards the end of my growing career most of my indica strains took roughly sixty days to flower, which means I could start a batch of clones in the lower vegetative garden. When they rooted, I immediately filled half of the upper floral garden with them. Then, a month later, I would fill the other half of the floral garden with a new batch. A month after this, I could harvest the first batch and replace it with a third. This way I harvested a crop every thirty days. Because the plants were forced so young they never got more than twenty inches tall at harvest, saving valuable vertical space. I turned the extra leaves from the harvests and mother plants into hash butter. I could harvest about a quarter pound of primo one-hit "wonder weed" per month and make two or three pounds of hash butter for baking brownies from the B-grade leaves.

You can tailor your garden's rotation to whatever clones you use. It will only take a crop or two to learn exactly how long it takes your plants to root and ripen, as well as how tall they will get and the average bud weight each plant will produce.

Chapter Summary

Windows gardens can be made more productive with one added grow light and reflective screens.

Closet gardens produce a lot of bud and are easily hidden, but often face problems with ventilation.

Natural light gardens are notoriously insecure.

A corner garden can be set up with relative ease, depending on the shape of the room.

Rotation gardens are cheap, require little effort and yield tons of great bud.

Terms to Learn
- Corner garden
- Rotation garden

Seeds and Breeding

Seeds are the natural start for almost all growers. The seeds you use contain all the plant's genetic information, which dictates their height, shape, weight, potency, and growth rate. If you know something about the plant the seeds came from then you may have an idea about what to expect. If not, you should at least use seeds from bags you liked. If growing indoors, try to find seeds from an indica strain, as these plants do better indoors than the common sativa. Outside, in the central to lower forty-eight states, sativas will do quite well.

Seed Selection

Seed shops and hash bars in places like Canada and Holland sell seeds for popular varieties like the Northern Light series, Blueberry, Jack Herer, 4:20 Bud, the Skunk Series, and others. New strains are being introduced all the time and something for everybody can be found. It is currently illegal to import viable cannabis seeds into the United States. Seed shops in Canada don't sell to the public; you have to order their seeds from a catalog and have them delivered. This of course presents a whole new set of problems.

If you don't have the means to go to seed shops then you may have to use local sources. As you may already know, most weed comes with seed. Due to poor dying methods imported marijuana may have lost a lot of quality before it arrives. Pick plump mature seeds; broken or squashed seeds will not germinate. Proper seeds could be brown, gray, black, speckled, or tiger-striped. Green or lightly tanned seeds will not sprout. Depending on the freshness of the seed, a normal sprouting time should be between two and 14 days. Small, wild, weedy seeds should be placed in a freezer for two weeks prior to being thawed and sown. Doing so will reproduce the effects of winter that they require. A simple test for

Germination 101 with Dinafem Seeds

Blue Fruit by Dinafem Seeds.

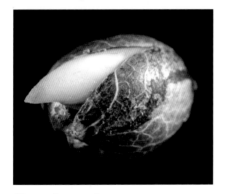

Taproot emerging.

Taproot extends from Dinafem seed.

Seeds are complete, self-contained, marijuana starting machines.

viable seeds is to place them on a firm surface and apply gentle pressure with your fingertip: if the seed squashes easily, it is dead. If the seed is hard and resists breaking then it is likely to be usable.

Seeds consist of an outer coat with a ridge running along one side called the raphe. One end forms a point, while the opposite has a roundish scar, called the hilum. Inside the seed is the embryonic plant, which consists of the first bud (the sporophyte), the first leaves (cotyledons), the main body stem (the hypocotyl), and finally the first root (the radicle).

Storage

Seeds should be stored the same way as buds: kept in cool, dark, airtight containers. Mayonnaise jars work very well. If you freeze your seeds, don't take them out from time to time to play with, as thawing and freezing over and over will kill them. Plastic bags placed in shoeboxes keep seeds fresh for about a year, if you use the kind that seals tight with a zipper rather than the flimsy little sandwich ones with the flap. Be sure to sift out all plant matter before storing; such matter may foster fungus and/or mold.

Lesson 1.13: *Seeds and Breeding*

Breeding

Breeding marijuana simply means to pick plants that you really like and crossbreed them to create hybrids that combine your favorite attributes. In reality, however, this is a lot harder than you think. When you cross two plants, there's a lot of genetic mix and match going on. Some hybrids may display the behavior you desire and others won't. It can take several generations of careful pollinating to stabilize the characteristics that you want.

Some growers use a haphazard method whereby they just choose plants they like and let them breed at random, picking the best plants produced and breeding them with each other. This method works well as long as the growers remove any substandard plants.

Danger!

Some growers and breeders like to post their results and breeder's notes online in various forums, and even on social networking sites. This can be fun, but be careful! You don't know who is out there, and anyone from a DEA agent to a rival breeder could take you for a ride.

Tip!

A good breeder keeps careful notes. Make sure you label each plant involved in the breeding process so you know what's what, and write down everything you do in your breeder's notebook.

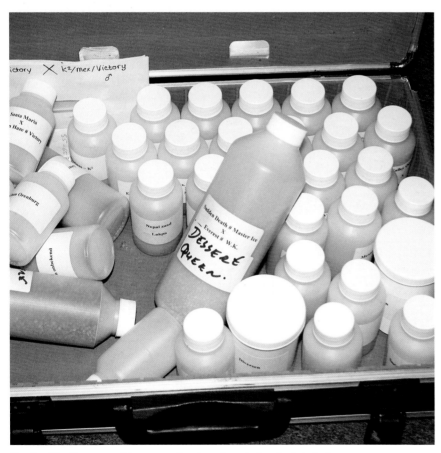

Seed collections must be properly stored and clearly labeled.

Danger!

For security, destroy breeding information when it is no longer needed. It might seem like a waste, but in the long run it's the best way to do things.

Tip!

When growing a specific strain, it is always advisable to contact the breeder directly and ask about your plant's requirements. Many seed companies have websites, so get a secure email account and start asking the experts some questions!

The keys to proper breeding are plant identification, detailed notes, and controlled pollinating. Tagging each plant involved in the breeding process helps you keep track of what's what. Detailed notes remind you which plants have which characteristics and which ones have been crossed with each other. Controlled pollinating is similar to artificial insemination; the grower collects pollen from a specific plant and pollinated flowers from another specific plant.

A single female may be crossed with many males by simply pollinating individual buds with pollen from different plants; one bud may be pollinated with

The expert breeders at Dinafem Seeds measure and observe every aspect of a plant carefully in order to determine its genetic viability.

Top Grade Strains from Three Great Seed Companies

Blue Widow by Dinafem.

California Hashplant by Dinafem.

Royal Haze by Dinafem.

Querkle by Subcool.

Jack the Ripper by Subcool.

Vortex by Subcool.

Chemdawg by Dr. Greenthumb.

Iranian Autoflower by Dr. Greenthumb.

Jazz #2 by Dr. Greenthumb.

Cloning makes reproducing your favorite plants quick and easy.

pollen from male #1, and another bud may be pollinated with male #2. Hardcore feminists may be happy to know that males are no longer required to propagate the cannabis species. By manipulating the light cycle, one can generate male flowers on an otherwise female plant. The pollen collected may be used to breed the plant with other females or itself. As the female plant has only female chromosomes, the seeds generated will eventually grow only female plants. To learn more about manipulating light cycles read the chapter on light.

Note Taking

Keep track of which plants have the traits that are important to your needs and palate. It will take weeks for seeds to mature, and in that amount of time it's easy

Tip!

Turn off your fans while you pollinate your plants. The slightest breeze can spread pollen everywhere, and you'll have a room full of pregnant, THC-less plants, not to mention the chaos it can cause to a pre-planned breeding program.

Lesson 1.13: *Seeds and Breeding*

Elements of Breeding

Pollen sieve.

Female plant ready for pollination.

Applying pollen via small brush.

to forget which mother is carrying which father's baby. It may seem like a tedious process, but since smoking pot can have the side effect of causing some short-term memory loss, it's sort of necessary. Keep this in mind (if you can).

For my own referencing system, I used a simple notebook, lots of twisty-ties, and some homemade tags. Each plant used would be assigned a number or nickname, and a tag would be attached to the plant's container. For your own system you should list each plant's attributes and which other plant it was crossed with. Keep the collected seeds separate and properly inventoried. If you can write small without your notes dissolving into a mass of indecipherable scrawls, keep your notes on the tags. For security, destroy breeding information when it is no longer needed.

A breeding program can be quite intensive; it can take generations to stabilize a reliable seed strain. When crossing two plants the results are called F1 hybrids. These can be quite robust in comparison to their parents, and can display many different attributes. The next step is to inbreed the best plants with either themselves or one of their parents (as awful as this sounds) in an attempt to stabilize the strain over the next couple of generations. If you're not comfortable with forcing your plants to be incestuous, you can also use the best F1 plants to make clone mothers.

Tip!

Use a small paintbrush or Q-tip to pollinate your buds – that way you can carefully pollinate specific buds and leave the rest of your plant seed-free.

Tip!

Identifying male plants early is important because if you leave them in the grow room, they will pollinate as many females as they can, which can ruin your harvest and also muck up your carefully-planned breeding program.

Bending results in a shorter plant with a row of excellent bud growth.

Controlled Pollinating

The idea behind selective pollinating is to carefully collect pollen from a specific plant and pollinate an individual bud with that pollen only. Try not to use mixed pollens, as it defeats the purpose of all those notes you took.

The best tools to use are a small paintbrush, some small paper bags, twisty-ties, and a water spray bottle. The kind of brush used for painting model airplanes would be the perfect size. If you don't have a brush, use your finger or, preferably, a Q-tip. This tool allows you to pollinate only a few select buds, leaving the rest of the plant seed-free.

Paper bags can be used both to collect pollen and to pollinate larger buds. To collect pollen, first remove the male from the garden to stop stray pollen seeding the females. You can place the bag around a branch that is still connected to the plant, but it's easier to gently cut a bud branch off and place it most of the way into the bag. Next, simply secure the open end of the bag around the base of the branch. Gently shake or tap so that the pollen will come free. Once you think you have enough, gently remove the branch from the bag. The pollen can now be dipped out of the bag and applied with a brush or your finger. To pollinate entire buds, simply place the bag over the selected female bud and tie the end firmly around the branch. Shake the bag to ensure the pollen coats the bud then leave it alone for about half an hour. Before removing the bag, spray it with water so that any pollen not on the bud will stick to the inside of the bag rather than falling out.

Chapter Summary

Viable seeds are plump and mature, not cracked or green, and should take no longer than fourteen days to sprout.

Breeding for certain characteristics isn't quick or easy; it can take several generations to stabilize strains.

Identification, note taking and controlled pollination are the keys to successful breeding.

Terms to Learn
- Raphe
- Hilum
- Sporophyte
- Cotyledons
- Hypocotyl
- Radicle

Growing

Sprouting

There is no great mystery about how to sprout a marijuana seed. People may tell you that the only way to sprout the magical things is to soak them in vinegar overnight, and then plant them in a pile of feces facing north while you dance around chanting phrases to the moon. This is ludicrous; they're just seeds. With a little push in the right direction, the damn things practically sprout themselves.

They do this thorough a process called hydration, which is the absorption of water. When dry, seeds contain about twenty percent water. The sprouts need to absorb an additional seventy-five percent of water to split the seed case and begin growing.

Once the seed coat splits, the first growth to emerge is the radicle, or taproot. It burrows downward to supply support for the plant, and then the rest pushes toward the surface. Once the sprout breaks the surface, the first set of leaves (the cotyledons) become photosynthetic and start producing food.

Sprouting Factors

Water

Ensuring that plants receive good quality water can be a problem for lots of growers. Tap water is notorious for being alkaline and/or heavily chlorinated. A gallon of distilled or bottled water costs less than a dollar at any grocery store. If necessary, use a pH adjuster to neutralize tap water for the remainder of the plants lives. Conversely, if you leave tap water sitting overnight most of the chlorine gas will evaporate out of it.

Fertilizer

When it comes to sprouts, weaker fertilizer is better; never use a full strength fertilizer on seeds or very young sprouts. They are babies, and babies need weak, simple food. The minerals in a strong fertilizer would actually remove water from the seeds or sprouts. I strongly suggest waiting until the seeds sprout before using any fertilizer.

Sprouts need immediate light.

Seedlings grow very quickly.

Try to transplant quickly.

Starter Mediums

Reliable starter mediums are professional potting soils, vermiculite, and perlite. Modern sprouting marvels like rock wool cubes make the process very straightforward. Mediums should always be kept moist, but not waterlogged or soaked. Use a misting bottle to spray the surface as often as necessary to maintain a constant dampness.

Temperature

Temperature greatly affects sprouting times; marijuana seeds can sprout at near freezing temperatures, but their progress will be greatly delayed if they do. If your grow room is cold, say below fifty degrees, then use a heat source to warm the sprouting medium. Professional warmers such as mats or cables come in various sizes and lengths. You could even just turn on the grow light and let it heat up the room—fluorescent lights are more cost effective than HID lamps for this purpose. Some growers achieve the same results by lining starter cups on top of fluorescent fixtures.

Light

After water, proper lighting is one of the most crucial elements to ensure successful sprouting. As soon as the sprout breaks the medium's surface, the leaves need light.

Tip!

For direct soil planting, use your finger to make the holes. The holes are to be one inch apart, and a quarter to half an inch deep. Plant one seed per hole, and the seed's pointed end should face up. And you're off and growing!

Always start more sprouts than you plan to use so you can pick the strongest for your garden.

Fluorescent bulbs make the best lights for sprouting. Not only do they cost very little to operate, but the cool burning tubes won't damage the sensitive plantlets. Up to one hundred starter cups can be sprouted under a modest fluorescent light. Keep the tops of the sprouts just under the tubes but never more than a couple of inches away.

Low wattage HIDs, such as one- or two-hundred-watt metal halide models, also make excellent starter lights. If using these, be sure to watch out for excessive heat from the bulb.

Natural light is the riskiest light source to use because of the security factor; the plants must somehow be exposed to the outside world. Also, the sun moves through the sky during the day meaning you may have to move the sprouts several times to keep them in the best light.

Sprouting Methods
Paper Towel Method
The paper towel method is a classic. Simply grab a clean plate and some paper towels from the kitchen, moisten the paper towels, and lay them on the plate. Spread the seeds evenly across the towels, making sure that they don't touch. Lay some more moistened towels across the top. Keep them in a warm place and make sure the towels don't dry out. When the seeds begin to sprout, transfer them to

Sprouting Hints
Seeds only need three things to germinate properly:
- water
- air
- heat

They don't even need light—in fact, they prefer a dark environment while they sprout.

Germination Techniques 101

Seeds between moist towels.

Seeds just before germing.

Taproot emerging.

OGA Seeds germination.

OGA Seeds new sprouts.

OGA Seeds sprout cups.

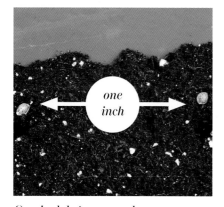

One inch between seeds.

Pointed side upwards!

Taproot peeks out of shell.

Lesson 2.1: *Sprouting*

starter containers. Don't let the taproots get too long, as anything over half an inch may not survive the transfer. The perfect time to plant is when the taproot is just starting to emerge.

The "Stick 'em in the Dirt and Water" Technique

A simple way to sprout seeds is by planting them directly in soil or a similar medium like vermiculite or perlite. This works well for the first time grower. Most outdoor and all indoor plants are grown in some kind of container flowerpots. If you don't have a starter container, simply take one larger containers and prepare it with medium. Water the medium and allow it to soak fo r long enough to ensure that it's evenly moist. Allow the medium to drain until only a few drops drip out when you lift it.

Tip!

Be careful fertilizing seeds and sprouts. I recommend waiting until the seeds sprout, and then using a very weak fertilizer. Strong fertilizers will kill a young plant.

Communally started sprouts like these need to be divided before the roots get entangled.

These lanky sprouts need more light to produce healthier, more compact growth.

Using your finger or a toothpick, poke holes in the medium an inch apart. Make the holes a quarter to half an inch deep and place one seed in each hole. Cover the seed with medium and remoisten the surface with water to settle the medium and remove any air pockets from around the seeds.

Starter Trays

When using these community starter containers, remember that after they sprout the young plants must either be thinned out or transferred to starter containers. If you don't do this, the roots will grow together, making separation much more difficult.

Starter trays are found at garden nurseries and cost around three to five dollars. They even come with a plastic lid that holds in moisture. Some come with complementary peat or rock wool cubes. Starter trays are also a must for rooting cuttings as they help make everything uniform.

The only real problem with starter containers is that they are usually no more than a couple of inches deep. As soon as sprouts emerge they should be immediately transferred to larger containers to prevent the initial taproot

Tip!

Fluorescent bulbs make the best lights for sprouting because they are cheap to operate, and they are not hot enough to damage young, sensitive plants. Up to one hundred starter cups can be sprouted under one modest fluorescent light!

Lesson 2.1: *Sprouting*

This new sprout has lots of room to grow in its container.

Chapter Summary

Water, fertilizer, medium, temperature and light all affect the sprouting time of your seeds.

The "Paper Towel Method" is tried and tested; simply lay the seeds between moist papers towels on leave in a warm place.

You can plant several seeds directly into medium, in holes made with your fingers, but once they sprout they must be transferred.

Terms to Learn
- Taproot
- Photosynthetic

development from being hindered. Clones should be transferred as soon as they become root bound.

Transfer sprouts as soon as they break the surface. For most plants something like 16-ounce drink cups are fine. In a week or two they will be ready to transfer to larger containers. Then use a fluorescent light source to raise the young plants until they are ready to be placed under a stronger light.

Use a very weak fertilizer to feed the plants. Professional potting soil won't need any because it has nutrients in it already, but sterile mediums need a 1-1-1 NPK solution.

Use seeds from smoke you liked. After all, why waste your time growing weak stuff?

Vegetative Growth

A plant's vegetative growth stage starts when the first true leaves appear and begin to use photosynthesis, and ends when the flowering process begins. Vegetative growth is the time during which the plants grow the fastest. Depending on its supply of light and nutrients a healthy plant may grow an inch or more a day. When growing indoors vertical space can be limited, so growers usually force plants to flower early while still fairly small. When growing from seed I don't recommend doing this before the plant is three or four weeks old. The plants should be about a foot tall and have at least six or eight sets of internodes. Clones can be forced as soon as they root.

Vegetative plants have certain needs that must be met so that they develop properly. The most important are light, nutrients, and strong air circulation. If a plant is receiving the correct amount of light it should grow quickly with an internode spacing of an inch or less. Read the chapter on light for proper lighting techniques, accessories, and sources.

Lights

When it comes to raising vegetative plants, including sprouts, seedlings, and rooting clones, smaller lighting systems offer big advantages. A high powered lamp can burn younger plants that just are not ready for the intensity such lamps offer. Regenerating plants and established clone mother plants also don't require high powered lighting systems. Instead, lower powered fluorescents, LED lights, and/or low to mid-range HID systems offer a better solution to these plants' needs.

These alternatives won't burn the plants or overtax your electric meter. More mature vegetative plants can handle higher powered lights and some growers

Thick Stalk Growth

Cannabis plants can become very large during the vegetative cycle if grown properly.

prefer to season their plants for some time under these systems before forcing them to flower. How large you grow your plants before force flowering is up to you, but most growers want to get from start to bud as soon as possible. I always tried to keep things compact and so I often moved vegetative plants to my floral garden as soon as they had passed the seedling stage.

Lighting schedules for vegetative plants are always on the long side. That is to say that they are longer than twelve hours of light per day. Plants grow the fastest under twenty-four hours of light a day seven days a week. But this can be a little taxing on electrical equipment so I always preferred to shut the vegetative garden down for an hour every day to let the lamps and ballasts cool off. In doing so, I extended the life of my equipment by years.

Shorter lighting cycles like eighteen on six off and even fifteen on nine off reduce electrical consumption and slow the growth of plants down significantly. I used this technique to keep cloned mother plants from overgrowing their space between cuttings.

Vegetative Lighting Cycles

Max growth Cycle: 24-hours/7 days a week

Recommended Rest Period:
23-hours on 1-hour off

Slow Vegetative Growth Cycle:
18-hours on 6-hours off down to 15-hours on 9-hours off

Lesson 2.2: *Vegetative Growth*

Growth Rate

Up to a point, the larger you grow your vegetative plants the more you can increase the final bud yield. The limiting factors to this include the amount of space you have to work with, how much growing the plants will do before they finish flowering, and the intensity of light you are using.

I have been guilty of waiting too long before forcing plants to flower. When I finished that particular crop I wound up with a bunch of gangly six foot plants that consisted of five feet of flimsy barren stalk and about a foot of disappointing bud at the very top. I should have forced them earlier, but at the time I was unfamiliar with the strain and the voracious rate at which these plants can grow.

Once flowering is triggered plants can double their size or more. Every case is different and you will have to do a little trial and error before you find what works for you. I can say that when just starting out, or dealing with an unknown strain, try forcing the plants shortly after they pass through the seedling stage and have just begun vigorous growth. You should be able to guesstimate what the next crop will do given your genetics and setup. Again, learning to grow is all about trial and error. It's ok to make mistakes as long as you learn from them.

Nutrient Formula Chart

Relative amounts of nitrogen (N), phosphorus (P) and potassium (K):

Sprouts: 0-0-0
Seedlings: 0.5-0.5-0.5
Mature Vegetative Plants: 1-1-1, 2-1-1, or 3-3-3
Clone Mothers: 1-1-1 or 2-1-1
Un-rooted Clones: 0-0-0
Rooting Gel or Powder
Fully rooted Vegetative Clones:
1-1-1, 2-1-1, or 3-3-3

Balcony grows are great, but be careful with your vegetative plant size.

Remove lower growth.

One short bushy plant.

Remove yellowing leaves.

Reducing the plant's growth rate is useful if you have to delay the start of flowering for some unforeseen reason and don't want the plants to overgrow your garden in the meantime. Growth reduction is also useful if you have to save electricity/money in a garden that is used only for raising seedlings, rooting clones or mother plants. Furthermore, reducing the growth is also a good method for allowing smaller plants in another garden time to catch up with bigger plants before they are all forced to flower at the same time.

Nutrient Diet

The right diet for vegetative plants would be high in nitrogen, which promotes leaf and stem growth. Worm casting tea, seaweed tea, or any water-soluble fertilizer should work well. Seedlings and very young plants prefer a low-strength diet. If the fertilizer is too strong it will burn the plants. Common safe formulas are 5-1-1, 5-2-2, or 10-5-5. For more info on plant nutrition read the Nutrients chapter.

You may have heard that certain strains of marijuana require different strengths of fertilizer. I have never heard of a scientific study to confirm or dismiss this, but anything is possible. Marijuana plants are extremely varied and considering the different climates that cannabis can be found in, some strains may have more or less needs than others. But, when it comes to growing your plants, be they sativa, indica, or a hybrid of the two, I suggest following the general "less is more" approach.

"Less is more" means keeping your fertilizer at a minimum to avoid burning or overdosing the plants unless they start to show signs of a deficiency. As long as the plants are growing well you're doing the right thing. I always diluted my fertilizer. If the side of the package said use one teaspoon per gallon every time you water, then I would use one quarter to half that amount every other time I watered. This lesson was learned the hard way from burnt roots and leaves, and lost plants and harvests.

You can tell if a plant has been overfed with nutrients because the tip of the leaf is shriveled and dead with brown marks advancing towards the untouched part of the leaf. Often leaves will curl downwards and draw in upon themselves. If this is happening, you need to flush the plant and stop giving it so much fertilizer. You are overfeeding your plants.

If you do feel that a certain plant has a nutrient deficiency, do not attempt to fix the deficiency with one big dose of fertilizer. I can't stress this enough. You cannot fix things with one fell swoop. A slow increase in nutrients is the best way to care for your growing plants. Too much fertilizer at once can kill your entire garden.

Lesson 2.2: *Vegetative Growth*

High Grade Strains in Vegetative State

Double Fun by No Mercy Supply.

Hydro by 420Clones.com.

God Bud by BC Bud Depot.

Medley by Ch9 Female Seeds.

Santa Sativa by Dinafem Seeds.

Zombie Virus by OGA Seeds.

Alpine Seeds clone mothers.

Thai Ko Chang in South Africa.

Santa Maria by No Mercy Supply.

Mr. Nice Seeds: Neville's Skunk.

Mr. Nice Seeds: Shark Shock.

Mr. Nice Seeds: Master Kush x Skunk.

So, add nutrients slowly over a reasonable amount of time, and see if the problem corrects itself. It takes a fairly long time for the nutrients you add to the soil or hydroponics to make their way into the root system, through the vascular system, and into the rest of the plant, so be patient.

Following the "less is more" technique, I recommend not using any fertilizer while sprouting seeds. After all, a seed has a tiny food reserve built in to help the plant survive through the first few days. After a couple of weeks young seedlings will benefit from a very weak nutrient formula like 0.5-0.5-0.5 or less. In soil based gardens fertilize every other time you water and just use plain water to keep nutrient salts from building up. In a hydroponic situation use the same 0.5-0.5-0.5 nutrient ratio in the initial water reserve and then continue to refill the reserve with plain water for up to a week. At the end of the week empty the water system and start over.

Actively growing vegetative plants can tolerate a stronger formula like 1-1-1 or 2-1-1 or at most 3-3-3 until they're ready to be force flowered. Mother plants are constantly replenishing the growth that is removed for making clones. I suggest using the 1-1-1 to 2-1-1 ratios. Freshly cut clones benefit from a rooting gel or powder and don't require any additional fertilizer until they are fully rooted and ready to be placed in the garden. At this point they are ready for the mature vegetative nutrient ratio.

Photoperiod Control

Photoperiod control is simply the duration of light and darkness during a period of time. For horticultural purposes this is usually a period of twenty-four hours in which a certain period of time is light and the rest is dark. For instance, a photoperiod of four hours means that four hours of the day are light and twenty hours of the day are dark. For the marijuana grower, controlling the photoperiod that their plants are exposed to is one of the most critical aspects of successful growing they must master.

Forcing Transition from Vegetative to Floral Growth

Forcing plants to flower is a simple process that involves changing the light cycle so that the plants are exposed to regular periods of darkness lasting at least twelve hours. This is called "the twelve hour rule." After about two weeks of exposure to this dark cycle, the plants should begin to flower.

The twelve hour rule is a simple one, but it can be hard one for a lot of

Lesson 2.2: *Vegetative Growth*

A beautiful field of ganja grown by Shantibaba at Mr. Nice Seeds.

red-eyed spacey types to follow. You know who you are. Simply put, once you introduce regular uninterrupted periods of darkness lasting at least twelve hours, the plants will switch to flowering. Because we live in a twenty-four hour world, most people use the tried and true twelve hours on twelve hours off schedule. This can be reliably managed with a low cost timer from a do-it-yourself store.

When you begin the flowering process is completely up to you. The only two things that you need to be careful of are stalk strength and your light cycle. Is your the stalk strong enough to support the buds? If not, you could lose your harvest if the plant breaks before ripening. Similarly, how will you manage to follow the

Clockwork Orange Haze by SinsemillaWorks is a cross of Orange Haze (Female) with DJ Short's True Blueberry (Male).

twelve hour rule for your light cycle? Will you remember to change the lights on and off, or do you need to buy a timer?

Most seed started plants are mature enough about a month or so after sprouting, some as soon as two or three weeks. Likewise, clones can be forced as soon as two or three weeks after being started. Clones can handle flowering faster than seed started plants because their stalk tissues are tougher and sturdier.

On the other hand there is nothing wrong with taking one's time and growing a larger plant. You may prefer to wait a bit longer and only grow a handful of larger plants. If you have the space, you can get some very large vegetative plants before initiating the flower cycle. You need to test these methods on your plants to see what works for you and the strains you are using.

Air Circulation in the Grow Area

Vigorous air circulation in a grow room has numerous advantages: it discourages insects and microbiological pests from settling in the garden, removes hot stagnant air, and exercises the branches of the plants so they grow stronger and thicker. Simple rotating fans can cool and circulate even the largest of gardens.

Be sure to prevent fans from blowing directly on plants, as this would cause windburn and kill the plants. Instead, bounce the current of air off a wall or have it blow over the tops of the plants.

Lesson 2.2: *Vegetative Growth*

Crippled Rhino by Stoney Girl Gardens.

Spice by Mr. Nice Seeds.

Pruning Vegetative Plants

Proper pruning during the vegetative stage will help ensure stronger, more productive plants that can support larger buds. By removing any undeveloped shoots or leaves that zap energy from the plant you help your bud grow better.

For the marijuana grower pruning is simply the act of modifying or removing underutilized or unwanted growth to maximize the plant's potential bud yield. This process starts early on in the plant's life shortly after it passes through the delicate seedling or clone rooting stage. Taking steps at this point will set the plants on the right path.

Outdoor plants exposed to sunlight receive consistent levels of light from the top of the plant to the lowest branches. This is awesome for them but most indoor plants have to rely on electric lights that may only be illuminating the uppermost growth. This means that the lower shaded leaves and shoots cease producing energy and food for the plants and become a drain on its overall growth.

Worse still, overcrowded growth can impede airflow which in turn encourages disease and pestilence. The depth that your light source penetrates depends on the power of the light being used and the distance between it and top of the plants. A small fluorescent system may only penetrate a few inches into the foliage while a 1000-Watt HID can effectively reach down two or more feet.

Generally speaking if the leaves and shoots are shaded or beginning to turn

Healthy vegetative growth.

Newly transplanted.

Nice early growth.

yellow and wither simply pick them off as close to the branch or stalk as possible. I suggest using a simple pair of sharp scissors to do so as breaking the growth off with your fingers can leave a jagged edge of tissue on the plant that is more vulnerable to infection.

Staking, Training, and Bending Vegetative Plants

Providing proper support and/or training for your plants is a valuable tool for all growers, especially those with indoor gardens. A support can be as simple as a single stake inserted beside a smaller plant's main stem, or an elaborate cage-like scaffold that completely encompasses larger plants.

Some plants can benefit from having their branches tied down because it can open the plant up to more light. However you support or train your plants, there are simple guidelines that can prevent problems.

Commercially available support stakes come in many lengths and materials. Bamboo, metal, and plastic stakes are the most common and can come in three foot to ten foot lengths.

Tying stakes to branches directly is best done with cloth strips because the larger surface area of contact won't cut into the plant's tissue like thinner twine would. Any strong twine will work well for latching a framework of stakes together or creating a boxing ring-like cage.

To fan out a plant's branches, a combination of cloth strips and twine works best.

Use a strong twine or cord to tie the cloth strip to a strong anchor like the plant's container or another heavy object such as a brick or exercise weight. Using the plant's container as an anchor point makes it easier to move or rotate the plant, but using separate anchors allows one to spread multiple plants out further and more effectively.

When doing a simple bend of a branch tip avoid using thin fishing line-like thread or dental floss as it will cut into the plant's flesh. I often used twisty ties or plastic zip ties to do these small jobs because if the cord is too thin and cuts the outer flesh of your bud, then infection and illness is more likely to occur.

Avoid sticking wooden and metal stakes into the medium, as the wood will eventually rot and metal supports may rust. Plastic stakes can be used in soil, but you run the risk of disturbing the root ball if there is some sort of accidental stake bumping. If you do stick the stakes directly into a container's soil, then sink them as far down as possible to provide maximum support and stability.

This technique works best for smaller plants that need only one or two stakes to hold them upright. When dealing with larger plants I always taped several stakes to the outside of the container and created a ring-like cage to offer general support for the plants.

The stakes should be about as tall as the plant's final projected height. This, of course, varies with different plants and is more predictable if you are working with a familiar strain or clone, so some longer stakes may have to be added as needed.

Another good technique is to grow parent plants to an acceptable size, then sex them, take and root clones from mother plants and then immediately force them to flower. The plants should be quite small but very productive, therefore avoiding any need to train or stake your plants.

Generally, single stalk plants may only need one or two stakes inserted parallel to the main stem for support. Growers should also remember that forcing plants early helps to reduce height problems, but of course with larger plants a grower could also, as discussed, use aggressive bending, pruning, and training techniques to control them.

Identifying Male and Female Plants During Vegetative Cycle

Normally you wait until the flowering cycle to identify the male plants in your garden, but the earlier you can sex the plants, the better. It is possible to identify male and female plants during the vegetative stage as long as the plants aren't

Original Seeds: Mazar

Early true leaves.

Lovely leaf shape.

Classic Mazar shape.

Original Seeds: Thai

Young plant is already leggy.

Gorgeous thin leaves.

Landrace Thai growing well.

too young. After a month or a month and a half of growth it is possible to identify them by closely examining the tiny pre-flower growths located at internodes under strong light and magnification. This is also possible if you have a very experienced eye, but that takes a lot of practice.

When I say these pre-flower growths are tiny, I mean it. You need a fairly powerful magnifying glass or telescope to see them, usually. There is no harm in having some fun though, so try to figure out which plants are male and which are female during vegetative growth, and then after you induce the flowering process you can see if you were right.

For educational purposes, male and female flowers can be described as follows: In simple terms males resemble the blade of a shovel or spade. They are flatter than female pre-flowers who generally look like teardrops. The females will not have the classic double pistil, or hairs as they are commonly called, sticking out of them until flowering has been induced. I was always about 80 to 90 percent accurate using this description, but I never removed a plant from the garden until I was 100% sure it was male.

Vegetative Growth for Soil and Hydro

Generally speaking soil-based plants may be a little slower growing than hydroponically-grown plants. This is because in a hydroponic system the nutrients and water supplied to the plants is immediately available and the plants can suck them up as fast as needed. I believe that the main reason soil-based systems are slightly slower is simply because growers have to wait for the soil to get a bit dry between watering to avoid drowning the roots. These little delays add up.

But this difference is not big enough to discourage anyone from using a soil-based system—after all, soil has its benefits, too. For instance, most growers agree that organically-grown weed tastes better, and a proper soil system can act as a buffer against accidentally overdosing the plants with fertilizer.

Vegetative to Floral Cycle: Nutrients and Flushing

A balanced nutrient blend can be used for the plant's entire life cycle, but adjusting the NPK ratios to provide more phosphorous will encourage larger and healthier floral growth. Common floral fertilizers are 0.5-1-0.5, 1-3-1, or even 3-5-3.

The best time to change the plant's diet is when you change the light cycle to force flowering. Prior to this change it helps to flush out excess fertilizer salts with several gallons of nutrient-free luke-warm water. It helps to add a single drop of liquid dishwashing detergent to each gallon. This will break the water's surface tension and allow it to better penetrate into the growth medium.

Chapter Summary

Plants in the vegetative growth stage need light, nutrients, a diet high in nitrogen and strong air circulation to properly develop.

When fertilizing, remember that "less is more."

Pruning and training at this stage will help plants grow stronger and more productive.

Remember to introduce any stakes or support cages during vegetative growth, before the plant is heavy with bud.

Controlling the growth rate of a plant is important.

Terms to Learn
- Twelve hour rule
- Forced flowering
- Photoperiod control
- Less is more with nutrients
- Staking, training and bending

These will become delicious Medical Edibles at All Good Medibles.

Floral Growth

It takes an average of two weeks for marijuana to move from vegetative growth to actual flowering. This transition period is known as the pre-flowering stage. During pre-flowering, the plant's sex organs grow and mature while the its overall profile also changes. The internodes begin forming a zigzag pattern of growth and the males may experience a growth spurt and grow taller than the females, giving them a gravitational advantage when dispersing their pollen.

Pre-flowering

Nutrients

Beginner growers don't have to do this, but if you feel confident, the diet of the plants could be changed to promote fuller bud growth. Flowering plants prefer a diet low in nitrogen but high in phosphorus. Don't eliminate nitrogen entirely because the plants still need healthy leaves. Remove any excess nitrogen from the garden by flushing out the system with a lot of nutrient-free water. Good NPK ratios to use are 1-3-1 and 3-5-3.

Try to avoid too much fertilizer during the flowering cycle as it can produce a chemical taste in the buds when smoked. Organic fertilizers often give the plants a more pleasant taste, but remember too much of any fertilizer will give a harsh taste. It is a good idea is to stop all fertilizing a week before harvest and flush out the medium to remove any excess fertilizer.

Lights for Pre-Flowering Plants

The light environment should be stable and well insulated. An unstable light cycle or some stray light seeping into the garden may delay or prevent flowering. Simple light timers ensure a consistent on/off cycle. Good growers go to great pains to insulate their crops from light pollution. Getting the correct dark cycle is one of the greatest stumbling blocks on the path to big buds.

Pruning and Training

Proper pruning and training will promote maximum buddage and even growth.

Identifying Pre-flowers

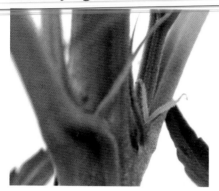

White "V" is early flower.

Early flower pre-buds.

Another early flower.

Twisty-ties can be used to slow down a tall plant while shorter ones catch up, and bending the tip of a branch will encourage a larger bud and thicker stalk. Support stakes or netting will provide support for branches while the buds mature. Plants with flimsy stalks and branches will bend or fall over under the weight of the buds. If a branch falls out of good light its growth is stunted, letting others quickly overtake it.

All pruning should be finished prior to force flowering. The plants will be going through enough trying to flower without being pruned like a bonsai the whole time. This last pruning you do should involve any lower shaded growth and underdeveloped branches that will tax proper upper bud growth. A great use for last-minute clippings is to root them and make some clones. This is very convenient if you don't want to maintain mother plants.

Flowering

From humble beginnings grows enormous beauty; the size, potency, and ripening times of your plants depend on genetics and environment. Sativa and sativa-dominant hybrids may take one hundred or more days to ripen, while indica and indica-dominant hybrids can take as little as forty-five to sixty days. The average time for most plants is around ninety days.

When the plants first begin to flower you will see tiny flowers here and there. The few weeks following this first growth prove to be some of the most stressful for inexperienced growers: the plants seem to take forever to finish flowering. Try not to panic though; it's only in the last few weeks that the buds will fully form and swell.

Lights for Floral Growth

The lighting schedule directly triggers and controls the flowering process and its maturation, or maturing process. When the plants are exposed to regular 12-hour dark cycles, certain hormones in the plants tell them that it's time to flower. Maintaining that regular 12-hour dark cycle for the duration of the flowering process is the key to growing healthy buds. This is why light timers are essential to produce premium buds.

The intensity and length of the light cycle directly affects the size and maturing rates of the plants. For a list of preferable light/dark cycles, read the chapter on light.

Always position the light source and plants so that the bud sites receive

Here we see some very dense trichome formations on an OG Kush plant by Alpine Seeds.

equal amounts of light. Try placing taller plants on the outside edges of the garden, and smaller plants toward the center. This way the smaller plants have a chance to catch up. If, by some small miracle, you get all the plants to grow to an even height, rotate their positions from the center to the outside and back again. This way all the plants get the same amount of light exposure and don't start out growing each other.

A single accidental interruption of the dark cycle won't affect the final harvest too much, but interruption after interruption will lead to a failure to flower or possible hermaphroditism. A lot of growers are unaware that there is a light source they can use around their plants without disturbing them. Marijuana absorbs all wavelengths of light except green which it reflects back making its leaves appear green. Because green light doesn't affect the plants you can use a green light source in the garden during the dark cycle without worry of doing harm.

Phytochrome

During the actual dark period, the plants produce a chemical called phytochrome. When enough phytochrome is produced, such as when they're exposed to 12 hours

Tip!
Be aware of your genetics before you start to grow. Sativa-dominant plants can become too large for many grow rooms, so you might have to bend, train, or prune them before they outgrow their space.

Pre-flower to Flower with OGA Seeds, Dinafem Seeds, and Mr. Nice Seeds

OGA Seeds: Pre-flower.

OGA Seeds: Early flower.

OGA Seeds: Full flower.

Dinafem Seeds: Pre-flower.

Dinafem Seeds: Early flower.

Dinafem Seeds: Flowering.

Mr. Nice Seeds: Pre-flower.

Mr. Nice Seeds: Flowers.

Mr. Nice Seeds: Late flower.

Lesson 2.3: *Floral Growth*

of darkness—the plant believes it is Fall and therefore time to flower. Phytochrome is photosensitive and is instantly destroyed by exposure to light. Even a brief flash of light is enough to ruin an entire night's supply. Light pollution during the flowering stage may prevent the plants from flowering, or even worse, produce hermaphrodite flowers.

Hermaphrodites

Hermaphrodites are very common in Asian strains, but the odd male on female flower or vice versa can be found with just about any variety of marijuana. One shouldn't freak out if they find one or two reverse sex flowers on a plant. But if the problem persists or gets worse check for light pollution during the dark period as it can sometimes trigger the condition. Most growers prefer to remove such plants from the gene pool, while other growers attempt to induce a few male flowers on female plants for breeding purposes.

Warning!

Even a brief flash of light is enough to damage your plant's supply of phytochrome, and without phytochrome your plant won't flower, so keep the dark cycle dark.

Close up of a Northern Lights cross by Alpine Seeds. The trichomes indicate that she is almost ready to harvest.

OGA Seeds: Staked plants.

OGA Seeds: Tied and staked.

Low Life Seeds: Tied and staked.

Other Lighting Options for Floral Growth

Maintaining a twelve on twelve off light cycle for the duration of the flowering cycle is the standard tried and true method for producing buds. But there are other options that a grower can advantage of.

The traditional way to speed up the flowering, or maturation process as it is sometimes called, is to reduce the amount of light hours to something like eleven on thirteen off or even ten on fourteen off. This will encourage the plant to finish quicker, but will produce fewer buds. Reducing the light cycle to something like eight hours or less on and sixteen or more hours off, will dramatically increase the finishing time, but could cause the plants to display some hermaphroditic flowers or in some cases switch sex entirely. This could prove useful in some breeding experiments.

A more useful technique that has been introduced is to utilize long light cycles. With this method the grower exposes the plants to a twenty-four hour on twelve hour off cycle to encourage faster maturation and increase bud size. The keys that make this possible are the regular twelve hours of darkness that maintain the flowering response and the extra time the plant has to grow fatter buds during the extra long day shift.

Timing

It is actually very common for seed-started plants to finish flowering at different times. Even if all the plants are the same strain, some will finish flowering sooner or later than others. This isn't a serious matter if you have the time to let all the plants mature at their own paces. Having identical flowering rates are more important in rotation gardens when a fresh batch of vegetative plants are waiting for the space.

Identifying Sex

Unless you are using clones you can never be 100% sure if a plant is male or female until it is actively flowering. This is when males are traditionally removed, or culled, from a garden. Always cull males before their flowers open and pollinate the females. They don't produce enough THC crystals to be worth anything more than breeding. If you want some pollen to generate some seeds simply remove some flowering branches and put them in a jar of water like a bunch of roses. Once the flowers open collect the pollen and use your finger or a cotton swab to selectively pollinate a few buds.

pH During Floral Growth

An improper pH level can lock up nutrients which will starve plants, so frequent testing is necessary to avoid simple problems. The complete pH range runs from 0 to 14, with 0 being the most acidic and 14 the most alkaline. Marijuana can only absorb nutrients in a pH range of about 5.5 to 7.5, which is fairly narrow. Either extreme is undesirable. For hydroponically grown plants, I suggest a level of about 6.2, but for soil-based gardens a higher level of around 6.8 is preferred. Simple pH testers are cheap, simple, and easy to use and are available at headshops, plant nurseries, and pet shops.

Fertilizer Problems

Mistakes happen. In case of an accidental fertilizer overdose the only way to save the plants is to remove a few inches of medium off the top and replace it with new medium, and then slowly run several gallons of lukewarm pH-balanced, nutrient-free water through the containers to flush out the excess nutrients. If successful, the plant will return to healthy growth. Don't fertilize it again!

Chapter Summary

Marijuana plants move from vegetative growth to floral growth in about two weeks.

In pre-flowering, a low-nitrogen, high-phosphorous diet may be implemented for fuller bud growth, but this isn't necessary.

Sativa plants might take over one hundred days to ripen, while indicas can take half that long. The average is ninety days.

Twelve-hour dark cycles kick plants into flowering cycles.

Terms to Learn
- Pre-flowering
- Flowering
- Identifying males and females
- Phytochrome
- Harvest times for Sativas and Indicas

Harvesting and Storage

Harvesting is as deeply steeped in myth and lore as any another aspects of cultivating marijuana. In reality it's a very basic procedure and one or two harvests you'll be an expert on the subject.

Most imported pot is brownish or golden. This tells you some things about its past. It was probably dried in piles under the hot sun, turned occasionally to ensure an even dry, then packaged and sent on its way. Sometimes while in transport the pot will sweat in the packages and be wet on arrival. Excessive moisture makes marijuana harder to smoke, and can also promote mold and fungus. Piles of pot act like compost heaps, generating heat within. This exposure to light, heat, and air quickly destroys the THC in the grass, leading to high CBN levels and poor potency. CBNs at best have ten percent the kick of THC. This situation, then, is of course undesirable.

The simple hang, dry, and cure procedure used to prepare most homegrown will produce a low CBN level and preserve THC, which is why seeds taken from a medium grade import bag may produce a higher quality smoke than the buds they were found in. This is always a pleasant surprise for the growers.

Plants grown from seed may not all ripen at the same time, especially if they are from varied sources. Seed buds should be harvested when seeds begin to fall out of the buds. Clones should all ripen within a day or two of each other.

Harvesting Supplies

Every grower pinches off a few leaves or buds while they wait for the crop to ripen. These are usually set aside in the garden and left to dry for twenty-four to forty-eight hours. This is harvesting at is simplest, but if you're lucky enough, the day will come when you'll need to cut and manicure some real buds. When this happens,

Thick Stalk Growth

Strains by Green Devil Genetics produce some incredible harvests. Trim, hang and dry your bud carefully for best results.

you will find the task a lot easier if you are properly prepared.

You will need a sharp pair of scissors, some drying plats or twine, some paper grocery bags, newspaper, some wide mouth glass jars or airtight plastic containers, and a safe place to hang the buds. Extras like rubbing alcohol to clean the scissors, music, and a few packed bowls or joints couldn't hurt either.

Selecting a Drying Room

The perfect drying room is dark, cool, drafty, and, obviously, dry. It's important to note that after harvest, light turns into the enemy. It will convert your precious THC crystals into worthless CBNs and CBDs, as will heat. Humid, stagnant rooms promote mold and fungus that will turn your buds into mushy slime. Rotating fans or a window mounted air-conditioning unit can lower the humidity, as well as cooling and circulating the air. Dehumidifiers should only be used when the room is unbearably humid, as they may dry the buds too quickly and lessen the smoothness of the smoke.

Danger!

After harvesting, light and heat become your enemies because they convert the THC crystals into useless CBNs and CBDs. Keep the drying room cool, dark, and, obviously, dry.

Hang dry your bud in a cool and well-ventilated place.

Tip!

Your marijuana is ready when it can be smoked in a thin joint without having to re-light it a thousand times. If it crumbles into dust — it is too dry.

Fix!

If you don't have any string or tacks to hang your bud on, try using the stalk itself. Just leave four inches of stalk on one of the branches you trim off and use it to hook over the hanging line.

Tip!

Don't dry on newspaper — the chemicals in the ink will transfer onto the buds and then your lungs. Not good.

Fix!

If you over-dry your bud, try placing a fan leaf in the jar overnight. In the morning the moisture in the leaf should have re-hydrated the bud.

Preparing for Harvest

Harvesting even a small crop will take a while. You'll need an area big enough to allow you to move around comfortably. Lay a sheet or two of newspaper on the floor where you'll be trimming the plants. Have your paper bags, drying plats, or hanging string ready to receive the pot as you prepare it.

Trimming

Select the plant you wish to harvest first and remove it from the garden. Remove and prepare one branch at a time by holding the base of the branch towards you with the top pointing away. Use brown paper bags to collect the leaves and stems you remove. I liked to use one bag for the leaf bits I wished to keep, and the other for the small stems and other worthless bits to be thrown down the garbage disposal or burned.

Start with the largest leaves first; cut or pinch them off, as this will give you a clear view of the buds before you start on them. Use a small pair of scissors, or even your fingertips, to pinch off the smaller leaves that stick out of the bud masses. Don't try to remove every single little leaf, just the excessive ones.

Drying

The initial drying period quickly removes the majority of water from the plant material. It takes around two to five days, with three days being the norm. The marijuana is ready when it can be smoked in a thin joint without having to re-light it a thousand times. It should not be so dry that it crumbles into dust when you handle it.

There are two basic techniques for the initial drying process: hanging, or drying plats. For the former, the plants are hung upside down from string or tacks. Plats are the cardboard case trays that cola and beer cans are shipped in, and if using these it's best to remove the buds from the branches and lay them loosely and evenly on the cardboard. Turn the buds every day to ensure an even dry.

Don't dry the bud on newspaper. The ink is not good for your lungs.

Curing

After the initial drying, the process is slowed down using plastic containers or glass jars with screw lids. I prefer the boxes; buds get banged around more in jars. A small harvest can be cured in a shoebox-sized airtight plastic food container. To increase the size for larger harvests simply increase the size of the box. Curing is

Lesson 2.4: *Harvesting and Storage*

Bud Storage 101 with Medical Marijuana Jars from mmJars.com

Organize dried buds.

Wear gloves.

Carefully place bud in jar.

Leave room for air.

Insert Oxygen Absorber.

Place gently on top of bud.

Close lid gently on jar.

Monitor temperature and humidity.

Perfect temp and moisture levels.

Well-trimmed bud is a great sight, but remember to dispose of leaves carefully.

the exchange of gases in the plant matter. Slowly curing the buds over the course of seven to ten days produces a smoother, better tasting smoke than just drying alone. It also preserves a higher THC level and prepares the pot for long-term storage.

First, remove the dry buds from the branches and place them loosely in the container. Leave the lid on until the inside humidifies, then remove the lid and let the buds dry out. Turn them to ensure an even dry. Once the buds dry out replace the lid and repeat the process. At first the buds will need to be aired several times a day, but soon they will only need to be aired once daily. When buds no longer require airing they are cured, and ready for long-term storage. Any marijuana you aren't going to smoke should be stored until you can use it.

Those of you who have never shelled out top dollar for pristine homegrown bud may be confused as to why it doesn't resemble the imported Mexican you're used to. It will have an intense green color with more red hairs, and lots of sugary THC crystals all over it. This is because it hasn't been compressed into bricks by a trash compactor

Danger!

Never smoke any bud covered with fungus. It can ruin your lungs and lead to all kinds of health problems. If you find any, cut it out and dry the buds faster.

A jar of harvested AK 47. Let air in once a day to prevent mold.

Tip!

Don't touch your face or eyes during the trimming process. Cannabis has a hot and spicy flavor, and can burn sensitive parts of the body if contact occurs.

Fix!

If you find that a lot of your bud gets moldy during the curing stage, then you need to dry it more before it goes into the curing jar or box. In addition, you need to burp the jars like Tupperware more often, and make sure that there is space around the bud for air to circulate.

These ripened clones will be harvested soon. Trimming, hanging, drying and curing will follow.

and banged around on a thousand-mile journey. That black tar-like stuff sometimes found in bricks of weed is actually the resin squeezed out of the flowers.

Check the buds daily for any sign of fungus or mold. It may start off as a fuzzy gray material, but a day or two later it turns buds into black slime.

Storage

Light, heat, and exposure to air will quickly degrade the potency of your grass. The best way to store pot for an extended time is to place it in airtight containers and store it in the refrigerator. A case of pickling jars costs about ten to twenty dollars at the local food store. If you don't want to use your fridge, then any cool dark place will suffice. Check the pot occasionally for mold or fungus. The same storage procedure is recommended for seeds. Once marijuana is placed in storage, do not expose it to air or light until you are ready to use it.

Plastic zipper-locking bags will keep your personal stash fresh for a week or

Tip!

If you cure and store your buds in jars, be sure to keep them in a cool, dark place. Do not forget to open the jar every day or two to "burp" them with fresh air which makes sure the buds dry out properly and don't get moldy.

Lesson 2.4: *Harvesting and Storage*

Remember to label your curing and storage jars like this expert grower.

Chapter Summary

The "hang, dry and cure" procedure preserves THC levels.

Dry rooms must be dark, cool and dry with low humidity and good air circulation.

Remove leaves and small stems, and then dry for two to five days on drying plat or by hanging the buds upside down.

"Curing" refers to the exchange of gases in the plant matter, achieved by placing buds in jars or containers for seven to ten days.

When the air within the curing containers becomes humid it is time to air the buds. This should be done daily until the buds are fully cured.

Buds can be stored in zipper bags in the short-term, or in jars in the fridge for longer periods.

Terms to Learn
- Drying plats
- Curing

two while you occasionally pick through it choosing buds. For reserve stashes, I suggest the pickling jars. Kept at room temperature the freshness will last around six months before the quality begins to wane. If your harvest needs to be stored for a year or more, do so in a small refrigerator rather than a freezer.

Quick Drying a Sample

Everybody samples the crops before harvest—for quality control purposes, of course. A few leaves or small buds can be easily dried using a microwave or electric oven. These samples may be a little green and less potent than slow-dried buds, but they will give you a general idea of what to expect.

For the microwave, use the lowest setting for thirty seconds at a time until the sample is dry enough to smoke, and for a traditional oven, set the heat at about two hundred degrees. Place the samples on a cookie or aluminum sheet, and check them every few minutes until ready.

How to Make Pot Butter

This is a basic but successful recipe that never fails to get you high. To make pot butter you only need a few things. The first is a pound of butter; get the real stuff. You'll also want a medium saucepan with lid, a two quart bowl, a spoon, a stove, a fridge, a mesh strainer, and of course some marijuana.

When figuring out the proper amount of marijuana to add to the butter I suggest erring on the side of caution. A first-timer would be wise to try only about an eighth of an ounce per pound of butter. Once you know how strongly this ratio effects you, it will be possible to adjust the amount accordingly to get the desired results.

Step one: The marijuana has to be dry; don't use any clippings fresh from the garden. When using B-grade leaves, let them dry thoroughly and crush them to a fine powder. Any bud material that you add should also be very dry and finely broken up.

Step two: Fill the saucepan one quarter full with water. Bring the water to a low boil on your stovetop then add one pound of butter. Allow the butter to melt then reduce the mixture to the lowest simmer.

Step three: Add the marijuana to the butter and water, stirring it very well. Cover the mixture and let it simmer for about thirty minutes, stirring often.

Step four: Pour the water and pot butter into the two-quart bowl and set it in the fridge. After a few hours the butter will harden on top of the water. You can simply poke a hole in the butter and drain the water out. Now you should have about a pound of greenish pot butter ready to cook with.

Part 2: *Growing*

Danger!

These things are strong! When ingested, marijuana is much more potent than when smoked, and the high takes a while to kick in, so don't be tempted to eat another one of those brownies if you're not stoned ten minutes after eating the first one. Too much can be quite incapacitating. I liked to save my brownie cooking until I had a nice weekend with nothing to do but relax. If you're not used to eating marijuana, it's easy to feel too high and think something is wrong. If you find yourself in this situation, just breathe, relax and turn the experience into a positive one. Hopefully you won't be alone, so tell your friends how you're feeling and pass away the time with some movies and good munchies.

Baking with pot butter is easy; just follow any normal recipe which uses butter, substituting it for pot butter. If you're too lazy for even that, you can simply melt the butter and add it to a packet of store-bought brownie mix. Be careful not to over cook them though; let them be nice and moist. They will be quite buttery and green tasting because of the large amount of butter.

But of course, there is always more than one way to cook a Kush or bake a space cake, and, with that in mind, I've invited the great people at All Good Medibles in Colorado to discuss their particular method of cooking pot butter, AKA Cannabutter. Trust me – it's delicious!

Step-by-step Instructions for All Good Medibles Cannabutter:

Here at All Good Medibles, we use our pot butter in a variety of infused products for medical marijuana patients each and every day. We are always cooking, and our Cannabutter recipe not only works great, but it's also delicious! So, get your chef's hat on and let's get started!

Step one: To begin with, you will need the following materials: a crockpot, ¼ pound of marijuana plant matter, 1 pound of unsalted buttter, 4 cups of water, a large mixing bowl, 3 feet of cheesecloth, a pasta strainer and 48 hours of cook time.

Step two: Start by putting a pound of unsalted butter in the crockpot.

Step three: Then add 4 cups of water. If your crockpot cooks a little faster, then you may need to add more water if it looks like the mixture is getting dry or may burn.

Step four: Add ¼ pound of marijuana plant matter, without the stems.

Step five: Let the mixture steep in the crockpot for 24-48 hours on a medium to low setting. The water is not meant to boil or the THC will begin to break down, but it does need to get pretty hot. Just FYI, your entire house is going to smell like cooking Cannabutter during this step.

Step six: Then you need to take out your mixing bowl and set the pasta strainer on top.

178 *Marijuana 101*

Lesson 2.5: *How to Make Pot Butter*

Step-by-step: Cannabutter 101 with All Good Medibles

1. Organize materials.

2. Unsalted butter in crockpot.

3. Add 4 cups of water.

4. Add ¼ pound of product.

5. Steep for 24–48 hours.

6. Strainer on mixing bowl.

7. Strain through cheesecloth.

8. Refrigerate the liquid.

9. The top layer is Cannabutter!

Danger!

When one eats THC it has about twice the effect and lasts about twice as long as smoking. I've seen hardcore smoker friends unable to get off of a couch or even form complete sentences for most of a day after eating just one overly-saturated brownie.

Tip!

When you cook Cannabutter it produces a very pungent smell, so be sure to have a well-ventilated kitchen. Also make sure your neighbors aren't going to call the police if they smell what you are up to.

Selection of medical marijuana edibles from Colorado's own All Good Medibles.

Lesson 2.5: *How to Make Pot Butter*

Step seven: Cover the pasta strainer and the bowl with the cheesecloth, leaving plenty of extra room off the sides of the bowl. Then carefully pour the contents of the crockpot on top of the cheesecloth covered pasta strainer. Let sit for about 10-15 minutes to allow most of the liquid to seep into the mixing bowl.

Step eight: Then gather the edges of the cheesecloth so it encloses the plant matter into a bundle. Remove the pasta strainer and wring out as much of the liquid from the plant matter as you can. It might be hot, so you may need to use gloves. It takes some strength to wring it out, so if you want an easier method you can pour the mixture into a french press style coffee maker and just press down on the plunger until all the liquid is out. Then when you can't get any more liquid from the plant matter, sit the bowl in the refrigerator for about 6 hours. Do not put it in the freezer or the water will not separate from the butter.

Step nine: After about 6 hours you will see a solid layer of green Cannabutter on the top, and a layer of waste water beneath it. Pour out the water, then add your Cannabutter to any recipe that calls for butter!

We use this every day at All Good Medibles while creating our delicious medical marijuana edibles!

Chapter Summary

When beginning, use only one eighth of an ounce of weed per pound of butter.

Once the butter is made it can be substituted for real butter in any recipe.

Take caution! Ingesting marijuana has much stronger effects than smoking it.

Terms to Learn
- Pot butter AKA Cannabutter
- Cheesecloth
- Crockpot
- Unsalted butter

Rejuvenation and Cloning

My first indica plant was a true beauty: a stocky little plant with twin colas, she was a compact, stinky little number I dubbed "Clover." Up to that point all I had grown were the best sativa I could find in my grab bags of seeds, and I had no idea if she was a true indica or not, but did she ever fit the profile. When that crop of plants was harvested I cleared everything out of my garden but her. I was ready to stop raising plants from seeds and step full time into the world of cloning.

I harvested her top colas and plucked the biggest buds off the side branches. I made sure to leave as many leaves and budding sites as I could, and then reset the light timer to twenty-four/seven. To further aid in Clover's regeneration I flushed her potting soil with warm pH balanced water to remove any excess fertilizer deposits. Then when her new growth started I gave her a low-strength dose of nitrogen rich-fertilizer. In two weeks she was making a full recovery; it was like she was reborn. The first few leaves were single bladed with smooth edges, yet many of them were twisted and deformed. This corrected itself within a few generations of leaves. Soon there were plenty of new shoots for me to clip off and root.

I now faced a new dilemma. I wanted to keep Clover as a dedicated mother plant and flower her clones as a rotating sea of green, but I only had the one small garden set up in my bedroom closet. For the time being I set Clover in a sunny window and set about planning my next step. What I decided to do became my standard garden for years to come, and it remains my recommended system for producing a never-ending supply of killer buds.

I constructed a double-decker system: two gardens stacked one on top of the other along the back wall of my closet. The lower garden was smaller and ran on some simple fluorescents. This was used to house Clover as a permanent mother

Room of clone mothers.

Carefully organized clone room.

Use a sharp knife to cut clones.

Clones grow very quickly.

Rockwool cubes start the clones.

plant and root her cuttings. The upper garden was much taller and at first was also powered by some simple fluorescents, but these were soon replaced with a mid-range HID lamp that flowered batch after batch of Clover clones. I go into more detail on this set up in the "Garden Examples" chapter.

The first time I made clones was after I had read about them in my first grow book. I used some small gravel rocks picked up from the parking lot outside, a cereal bowl, and plain tap water. I clipped four small shoots off a plant and stuck them in the bowl with the gravel and water. I placed the bowl near a window where it would be out of direct sunlight, but received ample amounts of indirect light. I simply poured a little water in the bowl every day or two and in a couple of weeks three of the cuttings had little roots. I had done this out of curiosity, just to see if I could. Little did I know that after refining this crude process it eventually would become my method of choice.

There are many benefits to using clones. The most obvious is that you know

Tip!

If you master the art of rejuvenation and cloning, you can set your garden up for perpetual harvests for years to come. Study hard and reap the benefits!

that the plants will all be female and therefore you don't have to cull any males from your garden. Second, the quality of the plants will be the same as the mother they were taken from. Other factors like a growth rate, flowering times, and disease resistance will also be predictable. The disadvantages are that clones sometimes have a longer pre-flowering cycle than seed plants, taking up to two weeks longer in some cases. Also, you do get the same type of high every time, but this can only be counted as a downside if you're really into variety. If this is the case you may want to use different mother plants to spice things up.

Young clones by the window.

Rooting Mediums

Rockwool

The king of rooting mediums, rock wool is pretty much foolproof and readily available. It looks like fiberglass, but really is granite or lime that has been heated in a kiln and then spun into thread like fibers, which are then pressed into blocks and cubes. I tried not to form an addiction for the stuff, as I hated the idea of being recognized as the guy who buys inordinate amounts of rock wool at the local head shop. Rock wool comes in one-, three-, or four-inch cubes, and larger slabs. It's so good that it can be used as the only medium in the garden.

Spray clones with water.

Peat Pellets

Peat pellets are just compressed hunks of peat that expand in water. They can be alkaline, so sometimes clones may not take. It's best to avoid these but if you want to use them, try a pH water adjuster to correct the pH level.

Perlite

Perlite is just crumbled up pumice. It works great as a starter medium, but can dry out very quickly so keep an eye on it.

Vermiculite

Vermiculite is puffed mica flakes that work just as well as perlite but also dries out quickly.

Rockwool cubes with clones.

Perlite/Vermiculite Combination

These two complement each other very well when used in a fifty-fifty mix. I consider this the best mixture to use as its a lot cheaper and less attention drawing than rock wool cubes.

Step-by-step: Cloning 101

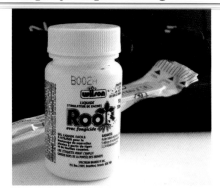

1. Rooting hormones increase success.

2. Cut one inch below internode.

3. Quick clean cut.

4. Cutting is six inches long.

5. Remove lower leaves.

6. Trim extra leaf tissue.

7. Cut off about one third.

8. Final cut below internode.

9. Dip in hormones, then plant.

Lesson 2.6: *Rejuvenation and Cloning*

Potting Soil

Potting soils are usually a mixture of sand, peat, vermiculite, and perlite. This is best to use in soil-based systems. Most starter potting soils have nutrients already added to foster rapid growth, but these nutrients are usually depleted quickly.

Fine Gravel or Stones

Gravel and small stones do the trick in a pinch, and because they weigh more, they don't tumble over as quickly as some other mediums.

Styrofoam

This is usable when broken up into little pieces or in the form of packing peanuts. The fact that these are often used goes to show that just about anything makes a good starter medium as long as it's inert and can stand constant watering.

Making Clones

The process of making a clone is relatively simple. Cut a shoot off a plant and insert it into a simple medium. Keep the medium moist, and in a couple of weeks the shoot will root turning it into a small plant. All clones made from one plant will have the exact same genetic profile as the mother; they should all grow and ripen at about the same rate. Practice on a few expendable shoots until you get the hang of it, then try your hand at making your favorite plant(s) over and over again.

Chapter Summary

Cloning involves taking cuttings from a plant and potting them to begin new plants.

Cloning ensures an all-female, quality grow.

You can use a variety of mediums to root clones. After some experimentation you will find which you prefer.

Terms to Learn

- Rejuvenation methods
- Cloning process
- Double-decker systems
- Rooting mediums

For a large scale growing operation that uses clones, you will need multiple clone mothers to ensure a consistent supply of clones.

Conclusion

All great things must come to an end, and this book is no exception. It's been fun, kids, and I'd to like to conclude with some issues that should be at the forefront of your mind as you move forward into your growing careers. I know you're all anxious to go out and apply your new skills, but bear with me just a little longer. I promise it won't hurt.

A Good Grower

In your hands you have a book that covers all the practical advice needed to start growing marijuana, but there is another component of growing that only you can control: yourself. I can't tell you how to live your life, but I can tell you some of the attributes that make for a good grower. I'm not talking about the technical stuff, but more of the proper mindset that you must have in order to succeed. After all, you could invest in the most expensive equipment and the finest seeds in the world, but if you don't have what it takes to be a clandestine grower then it'll all be for nothing. In my opinion the best qualities a grower can possess are the following.

Patience

It takes time to bring in a crop. Even with the most rapidly flowering plants in the world you're still looking at months from the time you sprout a seed to the day to take your first toke. Those final few weeks are really nerve-wracking, but relax: the best results come right at the end and are well worth the wait. This frustrating aspect of growing is the main reason I praise the application of a rotation system which will dramatically cut down on your turnover and nail-biting time.

Reliability

Most of us charge into new ventures bright-eyed and full of the best intentions, only to quickly lose focus and interest. Your plants depend on you for everything so if you stop taking care of them they'll suffer or die. My gardens ended up mostly automated, but if I didn't check on them routinely then all kinds of things would

Papa's Candy by Eva Female Seeds. Trim the sugar leaves, harvest the bud, and enjoy!

go wrong. I might have found such horrors as dried out plants and empty water basins, plants burned from growing too close to lights, or a failed ventilation system. Remember: if you take care of your plants they will take care of you.

Thoroughness
This is a big one. Being thorough is a necessity that runs through every aspect of growing; from keeping up appearances at all times to measuring fertilizers or pH levels exactly, and even cleaning up after yourself. It helps a lot if you're a little anal because many aspects of growing can be quite repetitious. After the hundredth time you dispose of harvest leftovers, measure out the proper amounts of NPK before fertilizing, or prune a plant it becomes tempting to cut corners. This is where mistakes lead to failures. Give yourself the time to develop a reliable gardening routine and stick to it.

Self Control
Perhaps you are one of the lucky people who live in some beautiful part of the world where it is tolerated or even legal to grow a few plants. If so, you're one lucky bastard.

Despite how green with envy I may be I need to remind you that you're growing something quite valuable and there are bad people out there that will want to take

Warning!
Patience, reliability, thoroughness and self control are essential character traits of any successful grower. You may need to grow as a person before you can grow your own stash successfully.

Conclusion

it from you, sometimes by force. Mastering yourself is the hardest thing anyone can ever do. It takes real skill and determination to keep your mouth shut and present yourself as just another average Joe with nothing to hide. It is horrendously tempting to share your secret or impress others. All I can tell you is that over time it gets easier to not blab your head off, but if you just can't keep things to yourself you should really reconsider the whole idea of growing. Pot is a fantastic and wonderful thing, but it sure isn't worth getting robbed or hurt for.

You should never find yourself getting lazy about your projected lifestyle. It may seem like no big deal to drag a box or two of grow equipment into your house on a regular basis, but the neighbors may disagree. I found it useful to sit in my garden from time to time and ruminate on what I could do to keep my skills sharp and my buds flowing like water.

The Pros of Growing

As you're coming to the end of the beginning of your marijuana cultivation education, let's take one last look at the advantages and disadvantages of growing. For most people, the benefits of growing your own marijuana are quite apparent. Until recently, high quality pot cost as much as or even more per ounce

Danger!

Remember, accidents happen when you get careless, so be sure not to let your guard down while you are producing your own buds.

X-Dog by Alpine Seeds is a NL x Chemdog cross with hard, compact buds and great resin production.

Marijuana 101

Quality genetics by Dinafem.

Cotyledons burst forth.

First true leaves appear.

Dinafem grow room.

Dinafem male for breeding.

Dinafem female plant.

Full flower.

Near harvest time.

Trichomes and pistils.

Conclusion

Autofem Seeds: Blue Kush.

Warning!

There are pros and cons to everything in life. If the cons of growing your own outweigh the pros, then you need to seriously consider what you are doing with your time.

Tip!

If you can't decide whether to grow or not, why not discuss it with people who have been there and done that? A great place to start is an online forum, like breedbay.co.uk or icmag.com.

than gold, so financially it makes quite a bit of sense to produce your own supply and save a lot of money. I very much enjoyed the fact that I had access to a steady supply of primo quality buds and didn't have to expose myself to any kind of outside danger or make a million and one phone calls to track down a new bag because my friends smoked me dry. Others enjoy the peace of mind in knowing exactly what went into growing what they're smoking. Some people don't like to ingest pesticides or live with the fear that the bag of weed they just bought was raised on a diet of chemicals in a cramped cage. Growing your own weed gives you

Gorgeous bud of Northern Skunk by Peak Seeds. This is an excellent strain with a solid track record.

Conclusion

BC Bud Depot: God Bud.

the choice to raise your crops in a completely organic fashion that would bring tears of joy to the eyes of any green stoner. On a serious note, some people grow because it allows them to see clearly for a few meager hours a day or improves the quality of their life medically. On the other hand, there are those who simply get their jollies off by having a secret garden—and there's nothing wrong with that.

The Cons of Growing

Whatever justification you may have for growing, you must always consider the downsides. The most apparent con to having illicit plants growing in your backroom is that your secret is as delicate as a soap bubble. If your grow is discovered, you instantly become vulnerable to moochers, thieves, and people with badges.

Tip!
Many modern growers have forgotten the classic, old school strains. If an old stoner tells you he or she has access to seeds or bud from Durban Poison, Panama Red, Northern Lights or Acapulco Gold, then listen to them! It could lead you to some great bud!

Silver Haze is an amazing sativa dominant strain from Sensi Seeds that was created by crossing Northern Lights #5 with Haze.

This is a beautiful landrace Durban Poison growing in South Africa as captured by the master growers from weed.co.za.

Tip!

If you are going to communicate with a seed breeder or company when acquiring seeds, then you should use a secure email account. Try hushmail. com or any number of discrete service providers to see what works for you.

The hidden downsides are less apparent. I can testify that growing gets in the blood and can take on a life of its own. Once a grower masters the basics involved in raising respectable plants they can find themselves wanting to see just how far they can take things. Technically there is nothing wrong with wanting to improve your plants, but if you find yourself losing sleep at night because you are trying to breed a neon purple and blue striped plant that is under six inches in height and produces three pound buds that smell like tacos, you may want to consider dialing yourself back a notch or two. Unless, of course, you pull it off in which case you will want to enter that puppy into a certain contest in Amsterdam.

On a more serious note I feel it is my obligation to warn anyone who has an

Conclusion

endless supply of high quality smoke to try and not fall into the old trap of doing nothing but get high all day every day. Before you know it you can find that years have gone by and all you have to show for it is the ability to make a bong out of an old door hinge and some chewing gum. In fact, I believe that one of the reasons that marijuana reform progresses so slowly is that most of us involved in opposing the government are completely stoned all the time. I'll stop now because I'm starting to sound like an after-school special, but remember this; you should be big enough and smart enough to weigh the pros and cons yourself and make the right lifestyle choices.

The Future

In Dante's Inferno people who tried to tell the future were forever damned to walk around the eighth circle of hell with their heads on backwards unable to see anything but what is behind them. As I'm a little superstitious I won't try to predict the future, but I will say that all signs point to the possibility of increasingly sane marijuana laws, provided that we overcome the same old hurdles that have always stood in the way. Those obstacles are the same ones that always seem to stand in the way of intelligent and socially beneficial reform in the US: money and power.

Believe it or not, there are certain people in this world who gain fortune and stature by carrying on the so-called "war on drugs." However, if we can continue to fight with everything we have then it is my hope that we might just one day be able to buy products made with American grown hemp, fill a prescription of buds at any pharmacy from coast to coast, or even buy a pack of pre-rolled joints in a pretty designer box. Until that day, I wish you the best of luck and hope that this book has answered any questions you may have had about the cultivation of homegrown marijuana. I know that a big part of who I am today was shaped by my years tending plants. Hopefully the knowledge I offer you will sow some very successful seeds, and perhaps cultivate a substantial amount of happiness in the process.

Happy and safe growing,
Professor Lee

Chapter Summary

Patience, reliability, thoroughness and self-control are traits of a good grower.

Growing marijuana is dangerous; the choice of whether to grow or not is yours alone.

Terms to Learn
- Patience, reliability, thoroughness, self control.
- Pros and cons of growing.

Resources

Seed Companies

BC Bud Depot
bcbuddepot.com

Brothers Grim Seeds
brothersgrimmseeds.com

Blimburn Seeds
blimburnseeds.com

Delicious Seeds
deliciousseeds.com

Delta 9 Labs
delta9labs.com

Dinafem Seeds
dinafem-seeds.org

D.J. Short
truenorthseedbank.com

Dr. Greenthumb Seeds
drgreenthumb.com

Dutch Passion
dutch-passion.nl

Emerald Triangle Seeds
emeraldtriangleseeds.co.uk

Eva Female Seeds
evaseeds.com

Green Devil Genetics
lamota.org

Green House Seed Co.
greenhouseseeds.nl

Kannabia Seed Company
kannabia.com

KC Brains
kcbrains.com

Mandala Seeds
mandalaseeds.com

Ministry of Cannabis
ministryofcannabis.com

Mosca Seeds
seedsman.com

Mr. Nice Seeds
alchimiaweb.com

Original Seeds
originalseedsstore.com

Peak Seeds
peakseedsbc.com

Rainbow House Seed Company
rainbowhouseseedco.com

Riot Seeds
riotseeds.com

Ripper Seeds
ripperseeds.com

Sagarmatha Seeds
highestseeds.com

Samsara Seeds
samsaraseeds.com

Seed Junky Genetics
seedjunky.com

Sonoma Seeds
sonomaseeds.com

Seedsman Seeds
seedsman.com

Seed Bay
seedbay.com

Resources

Sensi Seeds
sensiseeds.com

Soma Seeds
somaseeds.nl

Stoney Girl Gardens
stoneygirlgardens.com gro4me.com

Subcool / Team Green Avengers
tgagenetics.com

Sweet Seeds
sweetseeds.es

Vulkania Seeds
vulkaniaseeds.com

Weed World Seeds
weedworld.co.uk

World of Seeds
worldofseeds.eu

Supply Stores

BC Northern Lights
Pre-built Hydroponic Systems
bcnorthernlights.com

Humboldt Nutrients
Nutrient Company
humboldtnutrients.com

Online Forums and Information Services

420magazine.com
Excellent online resource and forum

Breedbay.co.uk
Excellent online forum and seed
source

Canamo.cl
Chilean Cannabis Magazine

Cannabisculture.com
Cannabis Culture News and Forums

Green-aid.com
Medical Marijuana Legal Defense and
Education Fund

Hightimes.com
Cannabis and Culture Magazine

Icmag.com
Online Cannabis Forum

Mpp.org
Marijuana Policy Project

Norml.org
National Organization for the Reform
of Marijuana Laws

Safeaccessnow.org
Americans for Safe Access

Skunkmagazine.com
Cannabis Magazine and Resource

Weed.co.za
South African Cannabis Forum

Weedworld.co.uk
Cannabis Magazine and Resource

Further Reading

Beyond Buds, Next Generation by Ed
Rosenthal, Quick American Archives

Hashish by Robert Connell Clarke,
Red Eye Press, 1998

Hemp Diseases and Pests by J.M.
McPartland, R.C. Clarke, D.P. Watson,
CABI Publishing

Marijuana Grower's Handbook by Ed
Rosenthal, Quick American Archives

Marijuana Horticulture Fundamentals
by K. of Trichome Technologies, Green
Candy Press

The Marijuana Chef Cookbook by S.T.
Oner, Green Candy Press

Marijuana Horticulture by Jorge
Cervantes, Van Patten Publishing

The Cannabis Grow Bible, 3rd Edition
by Greg Green, Green Candy Press

Glossary

Active System

A hydroponic system in which plants are fed water and nutrients via mechanical means. Includes aeration systems, nutrient film technique N.F.T., and ebb and flow systems.

Active Ventilation

Ventilation produced by using fans and/or connected ducts to exchange the garden's air.

Additives

Organic and inorganic substances added to soil to increase its performance. Such substrates could include perlite, vermiculite, peat and/ or sand.

Aeration System

Hydroponic system whereby the root ball is housed in an individual container filled with a non-organic medium. The container is partially submerged into a reservoir of water enriched with dissolved nutrients and oxygenated by a simple aquarium pump.

Aeroponics

Similar to hydroponics, but the roots dangle midair in a pipe or chamber and a pump and sprayer system mist the roots with nutrient-laden water.

Ballasts

Power sources specifically designed to run electrical lamps.

Bending

This is a simple process whereby a plant is intentionally trained to decrease its height and increase its yield.

Botrytis

A fungus that causes buds to rot which is bad news for plants and their flowers. Botrytis is usually associated with infected grapevines. Never smoke bud affected by any sort of mold, fungus or rot!

Branch

Woody part of the plant's structure that is connected to the main trunk of the plant. Supports leaves and flowers.

Breeding

Process whereby male pollen fertilizes a female flower to produce seeds. If performed carefully and with consideration, interesting new genetic material can be produced through this process, resulting in new hybrid strains of cannabis.

Cannabinoids

The psychoactive compounds found in cannabis plants.

Cannabis

Technical name for pot. Humans consume its dried flowers and leaves for medical, spiritual, and recreational purposes.

Cannabutter

AKA hash butter or pot butter. A cooking ingredient used to make cannabis recipes. THC is fat soluble rather than water soluble so the oils in butter are an effective agent to extract cannabinoids from leaf clippings and buds.

Chlorosis

Spotty yellowing or whitening of leaves. Chlorosis occurs naturally in older leaves and plants that are nearing the end of flowering, but it can also be a sign of pests, nutrient imbalances, and/or disease.

Marijuana 101

Clone Mother

A plant selected for its superior qualities that is then perpetually maintained in the vegetative stage, via long light cycles, to produce a steady supply of clones, all completely identical to the clone mother.

Cloning

Cloning is a process growers use to reproduce selected plants by removing small branches and rooting them. These new plants are genetically identical to the original making their growth rates and flowering times easy to predict. Clones are sometimes called cuttings.

Closet Garden

A small, easily concealed, and highly productive grow room design that is set up in, obviously, a closet or other similar space. Problems can include wiring and ventilation challenges.

Cola

A collection of buds that grow together to form a super bud. Colas are often the top most bud on a plant.

Controlled Pollination

Intentional plant husbandry. Simply put, a grower will take pollen from a selected male plant and then pollinate a selected female plant to hopefully produce offspring that display the best traits of each parent.

Corner Garden

A style of garden constructed in the corner of a room whereby two walls of the room form the back and one side of a garden and the other two walls are removable screens. This is a simple and very effective design.

Cotyledons

The first leaves of the cannabis plant. Contained inside of the seed, they emerge shortly after germination.

Curing

Part of the harvest process which occurs after the initial drying. Essentially, curing is the exchange of gasses in the plant matter which causes the buds to taste better and smoother when smoked. Requires seven to ten days and preserves a higher THC level and prepares the pot for long-term storage.

Dioecious

Plants, like cannabis, that are normally entirely male or female.

Double Decker System

Two gardens stacked one on top of the other. This system is popular with rotation gardens where growers have to meet the needs of both vegetative and floral plants at the same time.

Drip Systems

Hydroponic system whereby a pump sends water through a system of hoses to drip emitters situated at the base of each plant. The water trickles down through the medium and into a reservoir where it can be pumped again later.

Drying

Part of the harvest process which involves removing the majority of water from the plant material. This usually requires two to five days.

Ebb and Flow System

Hydroponic system whereby a pump and timer are used to periodically flood a tray in which the plants are situated. The water is then drained, re-collected, and then re-circulated at a scheduled interval.

Fertilizer

Nutrient laden substance used to feed plants.

Floral Growth

Part of plant's life cycle that produces buds and/or seeds.

Glossary

Fluorescents

The tube lights you see in schools and grocery stores. Come in a variety of lengths, wattages, and spectrums. They are excellent cheap and effective light source for beginners to experiment with. Fluorescents are especially useful for raising sprouts, root seedlings, maintaining mother plants, and young vegetative plants.

Forced Flowering

When a grower exposes a plant to regular twelve hour periods of darkness they will force it to begin its flowering cycle.

Fungus

A microorganism that can grow on plants and dried buds when they are too humid or moist. Fungus will ruin bud and can make one very sick if smoked or inhaled.

Hemp

Industrial name for marijuana. Does not contain enough THC to get you high, unfortunately.

Hermaphrodite

A plant mutation that causes male and female flowers on the same plant.

HID Lamps

High Intensity Discharge lamps are powerful lights used to grow cannabis and other plants indoors.

Hilum

The roundish scar on the bottom of a cannabis seed's outer coat. Basically it's the seed's belly button.

Hybrid

A combination of two strains of cannabis to create a new strain.

Hydroponics

Growing plants in a non-organic or non-soil environment wherein all nutrients are delivered directly to the plants by water in a systematized and sometimes mechanical manner.

Hypocotyl

The main body stem of the cannabis plant. Contained inside of the seed.

Incandescent Lights

Standard light bulbs that screw into common table lamps.

Indica

Generally shorter, bushier cannabis plants with broad, dark green leaves. They prefer cool temperatures and high altitudes, and come from the Middle East and central Asia. The high is typically more of a 'let's lay down on the couch and not get up for a long time' kind of high. Strains include Afghani and Hindu Kush.

Leaf

The plant organ that performs the most photosynthesis because of its large surface area.

Light Emitting Diode (LED)

Modern lighting apparatus that use less electricity than HIDs or fluorescent lights and uses only the light spectrum that plants need for photosynthesis.

Macronutrients

The major elements a plant needs to grow. They are Nitrogen (N), Phosphorus (P) and Potassium (K).

Maxi-cropping

Intentional removal of the top shoot of a plant to force the lower branches to grow and form a squat bushy plant.

Medium

The substance which houses a plant's roots, such as soil or rock wool.

Marijuana 101

Micronutrients
Elements needed in very small amounts for plant growth. They are Boron (B), Copper (Cu), Iron (Fe), Manganese (Mn), and Zinc (Zn).

Mold
Fungus that grows on plants or dried/drying bud. Mold ruins plants and buds by breaking them down into unusable and dangerous slush. Never smoke moldy buds!

Natural Light Garden
A garden that utilizes sunlight. Gardens can be situated in a window or on a balcony, porch, skylight or backyard. Security is always an issue with this style.

Necrosis
Dead tissue on the plant. Follows or accompanies chlorosis if untreated.

Node
The place on the trunk or branch where buds are formed.

NPK
Nitrogen, Phosphorus, and Potassium, the main macronutrients a plant requires to grow. They will always be listed on all fertilizer products as the NPK ratio.

Nutrient
Element needed for plant growth, such as Nitrogen (N), Phosphorus (P) and Potassium (K).

Nutrient Film Technique or Nutrient Flow Technique (NFT)
Hydroponic system usually consisting of pipes with individual holes for the plants to sit in. Water flows through the bottom of the pipes constantly so that the root tips can absorb nutrients from them.

Organic
Type of growing/fertilization style that does not use artificially-produced chemicals to feed plants.

Passive System
Hydroponic system, such as a wick system, that feeds the roots via capillary action rather than a scheduled, mechanized feeding program.

Passive Ventilation
Ventilation system in a grow room that allows air to come in and out as it would normally in any room of a house, such as through an open door or window.

Pistils
Part of the marijuana flower usually referring to the "V" shaped hairs on the female cannabis flower containing large numbers of trichomes.

pH
Stands for "presence of hydrogen" and is a measurement of acidity or alkalinity. The scale runs from 0 to 14, with 0 being the most acidic and 14 the most alkaline. Marijuana plants can only absorb nutrients in a pH range of about 5.5 to 7.5, which is fairly narrow. Either extreme is undesirable. Normally hydroponic gardens should have a level of about 6.2 and soil gardens should be around 6.8.

pH Down
Chemical used to decrease the pH of a medium or solution to make it more acidic.

Photoperiod
The duration of light and darkness during a period of time. For instance, a photoperiod of four hours means that four hours of the day are light and twenty hours of the day are dark.

Photoperiod Control
Controlling the duration of light and darkness in the grow room in order to force plants to behave in certain ways, such as vegetative and floral cycle behaviors.

Glossary

pH Up
Chemical used to increase the pH of a medium or solution to make it more alkaline.

Phytochrome
Chemical in cannabis plants produced during the dark cycle. When enough phytochrome is produced (such as when a plant is placed in the dark cycle for twelve hours of uninterrupted darkness) the plant believes it is autumn and therefore time to flower.

Pollination
Process whereby male pollen fertilizes a female flower.

Pre-flowering
Changes in a plant that prepare them for flowering, similar to puberty in humans. During pre-flowering a plant's overall growth slows down and the internodes begin to form in a zigzag pattern. Experienced growers use the pre-flowers to determine which plants are female and which are male.

Radicle
The first root of the cannabis plant. Contained inside of the seed.

Raphe
The ridge on the outer coat of a seed. One end forms a point and the other has a roundish scar (the hilum).

Regeneration
AKA re-vegetation or rejuvenation, this process involves harvesting the useable buds from a plant while leaving as many leaves and budding sites as possible. The lights are then reset to twenty-four/seven, the ideal light cycle for vegetative growth. The plant will return to a vegetative growth pattern in a few weeks where it can be later forced to flower for a second harvest or turned into a mother plant.

Rock wool
Growing medium made from granite, limestone or coke heated and spun into a thread-like substance that looks and feels like fiberglass. It is used to start plants for soil gardens, or as the principal medium in hydroponic gardens.

Root
Structural and nutritional organ of a plant that lies below the surface of the soil.

Root Ball
Large grouping of roots at the base of the plant.

Root-Bound
When the roots of the plant have filled a container and are constricted. Root bound plants should be transferred to larger containers or their health could be adversely affected.

Rooting Medium
Variety of mediums such as rock wool, potting soil and peat pellets which are used to house clones while their first roots sprout.

Rotation Garden
Grow system whereby a clone mother is used to provide a perpetual supply of young plants which can be matured at different schedules so that a constant harvest of buds is possible. A grower can harvest a crop every thirty days with practice. This is a very effective system.

Ruderalis
A hardy species of cannabis originating in Russia that flowers based on age rather than lighting schedule. True Ruderalis plants are essentially worthless, but some professional breeders have used them to create compact hybrids that are quick to flower.

Sativa
Generally larger cannabis plants with long, narrow, light green leaves. They take longer to mature, prefer hot and humid climates, and can produce several pounds of buds per plant when grown outdoors. The high is typically more cerebral and alert. Strains include Mexican, Colombian, Jamaican, African, Asian and Indian (ie tropical climates).

Screen of Green (ScrOG)

Growing style in which plants are trained to grow to an even height by a combination of careful pruning and bending, as well as the use of a screen (often chicken wire) which is placed over the plants, forcing them to grow to a specific height and shape. This is a great technique for growers with limited vertical space, as well as growers using fluorescent lights.

Sea of Green (SOG)

Growing style in which all plants are trained to grow to an even height so that when seen from above they resemble a calm green ocean.

Secondary Nutrients

Elements needed in less abundance for plant growth than the macronutrients. They are Calcium (Ca), Sulfur (S), and Magnesium (Mg).

Sinsemilla

Unfertilized female cannabis plants. Because the female flowers are never pollinated the ovaries swell with THC resin instead of seeds.

Sporophyte

The first bud of a cannabis plant. Contained inside of the seed.

Staking

Using stakes to support plants. This is especially important during the floral stage when plants are heavy with buds.

Stem

Structural part of the plant. Holds the plant up, and is divided into nodes and internodes.

Taproot

Also called a radicle, this is the first growth to emerge from the germinating seed and forms the main root as it grows.

Tetrahydrocannabinol (THC)

The main psychoactive chemical that gets one high.

Training

Process whereby a plant is tied down in a specific direction to increase its yield and control its shape.

Trichomes

Tiny white crystals that form on cannabis flowers and leaves. Generally speaking the more trichomes a plant has the higher its THC levels are.

Trimming

Part of the harvest process whereby removing stems and leaves from the buds.

Twelve Hour Rule

Rule which dictates that if a cannabis plant is exposed to at least twelve hours of uninterrupted darkness on a regular basis for about two weeks, it will begin its floral cycle.

Vegetative Growth

Part of plant's life cycle where it grows the fastest. This comprises of the time between the plant's first true leaves appearing and the beginning of the floral cycle.

Wick System

Simple hydroponic system whereby the roots are fed via a cord in a nutrient bath leading to the roots, ie capillary action.

Window Garden

A garden that utilizes a window as its main light source. Reflective screens can reinforce the light's power, and a simple set of thick curtains and/or a spotlight can be used to augment the light schedule. Security is always important in this type of setup.

Index

Marijuana 101

Index

Index